365 DAYS OF
SLOW-COOKING RECIPES

Emma Katie

Copyright © 2016 Emma Katie

Check out more books by Emma Katie at:
www.amazon.com/author/emmakatie

ISBN-13: 978-1539581420

Contents

Dinner Recipes 131

Desserts & Beverages

About

After some researching, we have figured out that healthy eating is all about feeling great, having more energy, stabilizing your mood, and keeping yourself as healthy as possible, all of which can be achieved by learning some nutrition basics and using them in a way that works for you.

This eBook will be handy for everybody who is looking for a healthier life, taking in consideration the favorable circumstances that slow cooking gives, like the extended cooking times that permit better circulation of flavors in numerous recipes. Tough meats, such as chuck roasts or steaks and stew beef, are softened through the long cooking procedure.

Comfort! A slow cooker can normally be left unattended throughout the day for most recipes, so you can put recipe ingredients in it, before going to work and get back to a feast.

Introduction

Prohibitive eating regimens don't work in the long run, we all know, and with the exception of a couple of lost pounds, they don't do much as far as enhancing your general wellbeing or appearance. This is the reason I'm not into eating less and I incline toward a healthy lifestyle that permits me to effectively manage my weight, as well as to enjoy delicious meals, without worrying over my weight and wellbeing.

My accumulation of recipes broadened rapidly, so I need to share some of my most loved slow cooker recipes with you. They're tried and true, flavorful and healthy, so on the off chance that you appreciate tasty, saucy, rich, mouthwatering dishes, this eBook is unquestionably for you.

Don't hesitate to explore different ways to use different ingredients and to conform the taste, depending upon your particular inclination. However, stay with the suggested cooking times and ingredient amounts. Preparing food using the slow cooker requires more patience, but the reward is definitely worth the time and effort.

Happy cooking, and if you enjoy this eBook, make sure to connect with me via social media and to check the other publications from Recipes365.net.

Advantages of Slow Cooking

It is summer and I am falling in love again and I thank my friend for acquainting me with my new love: My astonishing, high-end, sparkly, brand new slow cooker. I'd generally had slow-cooker dreams. You know, getting back home to meat and vegetable yummy stews after a difficult day at work. I will now introduce you to this new great love that I found.

Efficiency is a major advantage. Put your ingredients in a slow cooker in the morning, let them cook throughout the day, and return home at night to a hot, ready to-consume, one-pot feast. Another point is that slow cooking makes it good for dieting. High temperatures do two things to nourishment: break down their supplements (cancer prevention agents, vitamins, and minerals) and create unhealthy chemical compounds that have been related to diseases like, diabetes, Alzheimer's illness, and renal inconveniences. Cooking on low heat or temperature permits meals to keep in their supplements and hazardous chemicals are not generated. Slow cooking, likewise saves the freshness and pleasantly flavors. Your food does not overcook or blaze. Also ultimately, you save cash three ways:

1) Ingredients used to make the best slow cooker meals (stews, soups, rice, and casseroles) are usually inexpensive.

2) The quantity is such that you can re-heat and heat for more than a day.

3) You save on gas and electricity and also on water as you are just using one pot.

WHAT YOU NEED TO KNOW TO COOK IN YOUR SLOW COOKER?

What could be less demanding than tossing the ingredients into a slow cooker in the morning and getting back to a hot, cooked dinner? Before you get started, here are a few things you have to know:

Slow cookers can plan practically any sort of feast you can envision, including the accompanying side dishes, breads, and sweets. You don't need to worry over the food; there's no need for steady attention or mixing. (Now that it's been brought up, unless the recipe states otherwise, you should not lift the cover while cooking because the heat that escapes adds almost another 30 minutes to the cooking time.)

Slow cookers are perfect for making soups and stews, and they're especially useful for dishes that call for harder, economical cuts of meat. While that fact remains, you can even use your slow cooker to prepare side dishes and sweets, as well. This is particularly useful in case you're entertaining guests and your oven is being used to make another dish. All things considered, you can utilize your slow cooker as an alternate stove or burner.

To make cleanup less demanding, spray the container with nonstick cooking spray before adding the food.

Meats won't tan in the slow cooker, so recipes with sautéed meat need to have the meat tanned in a skillet before putting it in the slow cooker.

Slow cooking doesn't lose to the extent as tried and true cooking techniques, so (in spite of the fact that you may be enticed) don't add more liquid to the cooker than the recipe calls for.

Keep in mind that cooking times in all recipes are close estimations. A few elements can influence cooking time (your slow cooker's eccentricities, what amount of food is in the cooker, the humidity, the temperature of the ingredients when you include them)

Don't keep your completed dish in the slow cooker for long. It will keep on cooking for a while, which could overcook the food; then, as the slow cooker cools, the meal won't stay hot enough to avert microbe development. Similarly, don't utilize your slow cooker for warming; the cooker just slowly achieves cooking temperature, which gives microscopic organisms the opportunity to develop.

Liquids

Use about half the recommended amount of liquid in slow cooking. One mug liquid is enough for any recipe unless it contains rice or pasta. Example: If a recipe calls for 2 cans beef broth, 1 will do.

Herbs & Spices

In slow cookers flavored leaves or entire herbs and spices are used, yet their flavor force may build, so use just use half the recommended amount, and afterward adjust to suit your family's taste. In the event that you use ground herbs and spices, include an hour ago of cooking.

Quantities

The amount of meat, poultry and vegetables may be diminished without influencing flavor, particularly vegetables! In the event there is uncertainty, cut the recipe down the middle.

TIPS FOR SLOW COOKING DIFFERENT FOODS

Dairy products: Full-fat dairy items are more steady and don't sour as effortlessly as low fat milk items. In this eBook, milk items are added close to the end of cooking time and consolidated with cornstarch to build security. Evaporated milk and canned cream soups are exceptionally steady and might be added to the slow cooker at the start of cooking time.

Dried lentils and split peas: Do not require soaking and can be added to the recipe at the start of cooking time.

Vegetables: High-moisture vegetables, for example, yellow winter squash or zucchini, cook more rapidly than root vegetables, so cut into bigger pieces or include during the last 30 minutes of cooking time.

Dried beans: Will cook in soups and stews with abundant liquid in 7 to 8 hours on high; they don't have to be pre-soaked. Corrosive ingredients, for example, tomatoes and vinegar, keep beans from becoming tender, so add the acidic ingredients close to the end of cooking time after the beans are tender.

Pasta: Dried pasta ought to be cooked still somewhat firm and added to the slow cooker in the last 15 to 20 minutes cooking time; little soup pasta, for example, acini de pepe or orzo might be included, uncooked, in the last 20 to 30 minutes cooking time. Fresh pastas can be included, uncooked, in the last 15 to 20 minutes of cooking time. Fluid (stock, water, wine)—Aids in high temperature exchange and encourages cooking.

Meats: Less delicate cuts of meat, for example, pork shoulder, beef rump, and chuck roast, are ideal for long, slow cooking. Ground meats need to be cooked and disintegrated with a fork before adding to the slow cooker; else they will cook into a "bunch" in the slow cooker. Other cuts don't have to be browned; the distinction in appearance and flavor is minimal, and not browning saves time and dirty pots and pans.

Seafood: Include shellfish (shrimp, scallops, shellfishes) and bits of fish (salmon, red snapper, fish, haddock) in the last 10 to 15 minutes of cooking time, depending on the amount and thickness of the fish.

Rice: Only converted long-grain rice can be cooked successfully in the slow cooker; be sure the recipe has plenty of liquid and add the uncooked rice during the last 1½ to 2 hours of cooking time. Other types of rice, such as jasmine, basmati, or brown, should be cooked and added near the end of cooking time.

Frozen vegetables: Defrost and add to the slow cooker in the last 15 to 20 minutes of cooking time to hold best composition.

Herbs: Include crisp herbs at the end for ideal shade and flavor. Include ground and dried herbs at starting, adding more to taste at the end, if necessary.

BENEFITS BEYOND NUTRIENTS

The advantages of slow cooking broaden past expanding the bio availability of supplements in plant nourishment. In the event that you cook meat in a fluid at low high temperature, you can help decrease the amount of cell-harming mixes known as AGEs (advanced glycation end products) that are generated in the meat by 50 percent, while searing or barbecuing. That is the reason slow cooking is arguably one of the most secure approaches to cook meats, as AGEs commonly found in charred and grilled meats have been linked with inflammation, diabetes, heart disease and cancer.

Breakfast Recipes

Creamy Oatmeal with Dried Fruit

Ingredients

1/4 cup Apple juice
1/4 cup pure maple syrup
1/4 cup raisins
1/4 tsp. of ground ginger
½ tsp. Salt
2 cups rolled oats
1 (12-oz) can evaporated milk

Method

Grease the slow cooker liberally with vegetable oil spray or melted butter. Then you have to add the oats, evaporated milk, apple juice, maple syrup, apricots, cranberries, raisins, ginger, and salt to the slow cooker. Stir the whole thing well.

Cook on a low heat for 5 to 7 hours or on high heat for 2½ to 3 hours or until the oatmeal is soft and mixture is creamy. Stir halfway through cooking time. Serve immediately. Enjoy!

Cornmeal Porridge with Raspberries

Ingredients

3½ cups water
1 (12-oz.) can evaporated Milk
¼ cup firmly packed light Brown sugar
1 cup yellow cornmeal or polenta
¼ tsp. ground cinnamon
¼ tsp. ground nutmeg
Pinch of salt
1 cup mascarpone cheese
1 pint fresh raspberries, rinsed

Method

Grease the slow cooker liberally with vegetable oil spray or melted butter. Combine the water, evaporated milk, and brown sugar in the slow cooker. Stir well to dissolve sugar. Whisk in cornmeal, cinnamon, nutmeg, and salt.

Cook on low for 6 to 8 hours or on high for 3 to 4 hours or until mixture is very thick. Stir every few hours after the mix comes to a boil. If cooking on high, reduce the heat to low. Stir in mascarpone and whisk well. Gently fold in raspberries, and cook for 5 minutes to warm the berries. Serve immediately. Enjoy!

Hot Apple Muesli

Ingredients

4 Granny Smith apples, peeled, cored, and diced
¾ tsp. ground cinnamon
¼ cup granulated sugar
2 tbsp. freshly squeezed lemon juice
2 cups muesli cereal
½ cup raisins
4 tbsp. Unsalted butter, melted

Method

Grease the inside of the slow cooker liberally with vegetable oil spray. Place the apples in a mixing bowl, and toss with cinnamon, sugar, and lemon juice until evenly coated. Stir in muesli cereal and raisins. Transfer mixture to the slow cooker. Drizzle melted butter on the top. Cook on low for 6 to 8 hours or on high for 3 to 4 hours or until apples are tender. Serve immediately.
Variation: This recipe works equally well with your favorite granola in place of the muesli, and feel free to substitute peaches for the apples. Enjoy!

Scrambled Eggs for a Crowd

Ingredients

3 dozen large eggs
1 cup sour cream
Salt and freshly ground black pepper

Method

Grease the inside of the slow cooker liberally with vegetable oil spray or melted butter. Whisk the eggs with sour cream, and season with salt and pepper. Pour mixture into the slow cooker.
Cook on low for 2 to 4 hours or until the eggs are set. Stir the eggs after 1½ hours of cooking to break up the cooked egg portion. Serve hot. Enjoy!

Spinach and Cheese Strata

Ingredients

3 tbsp. unsalted butter
1 medium onion, peeled and diced
6 large eggs, lightly beaten
2 cups whole milk
1 tbsp. Herbs de Provence (Or use a mixture of 1 tsp. dried thyme, 1 tsp. dried rosemary and 1 tsp. Dried basil)
Salt and freshly ground black pepper
1 lb. loaf white bread, broken into small pieces
1 (10-oz.) package frozen chopped spinach, thawed
1½ cups grated mozzarella cheese

Method

Heat the butter in a small skillet over medium-high heat. Add the onion and cook, stirring frequently, for 3 minutes or until the onion is translucent. Remove the pan from the heat and set aside. Grease the inside of the slow cooker liberally with vegetable oil spray or melted butter.

Combine the eggs, milk, herbs de Provence, salt, and pepper in a large mixing bowl, and whisk well. Add bread pieces to the bowl, and stir so bread absorbs the egg mixture.

Place spinach in a sieve and press with the back of a spoon to extract as much liquid as possible. Add onion, spinach, and cheese to bread mixture and stir well. Transfer mixture to the slow cooker.

Cook on low for 4 to 6 hours or until the mixture is puffed and an instant-read thermometer inserted in the center reads 165°F. Serve immediately.

Variation: Try this with chopped broccoli or chopped asparagus and cheddar cheese instead of spinach and mozzarella. Enjoy!

Sausage, Apple, and Sage Raisin Bread Strata

Ingredients

1 large Golden Delicious apple
8 large eggs
3½ cups whole milk
Salt and freshly ground black pepper
1 cup grated mozzarella cheese
¾ lb. loaf raisin bread, cut into ½-in. cubes

¾ lb. bulk breakfast sausage
2 tbsp., unsalted butter
1 small onion, peeled and diced
3 tbsp. granulated sugar
¼ cup chopped fresh sage or 1 tbsp. dried
½ tsp. ground cinnamon

Method

Peel the apple and cut into quarters. Discard core and slice quarters into thin slices. Grease the inside of the slow cooker liberally with vegetable oil spray. Combine the eggs, milk, salt, and pepper in a mixing bowl, and whisk well. Stir in mozzarella cheese and bread cubes, and keep stirring so bread absorbs egg mixture.

Place a large skillet over medium-high heat. Add the sausages, breaking up the lumps with a fork. Cook the sausages, stirring frequently, for 5 minutes or until browned. Remove the sausages from the pan with a slotted spoon and add to bread mixture. Discard sausage grease. Place the skillet on the stove and heat on medium heat. Add butter and onion and sauté until the onions are tender and translucent. Add in the apple, sugar, sage, and cinnamon to the skillet and keep cooking until the apple is tender. Mix in the contents of the pan into the bread mix and transfer the mixture to the slow cooker.

Cook on low for 4 to 6 hours or until the mixture is puffed and an instant-read thermometer inserted in the center reads 165°F. Serve immediately.

Variation: If raisin bread isn't available, use a ¾-pound loaf French or Italian bread and add ½ cup raisins and an additional ½ tsp. cinnamon to custard mixture. Enjoy!

Blueberry French Toast Strata

Ingredients

8 large eggs
3½ cups whole milk
Salt
1 cup granulated sugar
1 tbsp. grated lemon zest
1 tsp. pure vanilla extract
¾ lb. loaf challah, Portuguese sweet bread, or white bread, cut into ½-in. cubes
1 pint fresh blueberries, rinsed, or 2 cups dry-packed frozen blueberries, thawed

Method

Grease the inside of the slow cooker liberally with vegetable oil spray or melted butter. Combine the eggs, milk, salt, sugar, lemon zest, and vanilla extract in a mixing bowl, and whisk well. Add bread cubes, and stir so bread absorbs egg mixture. Add blueberries, and stir again. Transfer mixture to the slow cooker.

Cook on low for 4 to 6 hours or until the mixture is puffed and an instant-read thermometer inserted in the center reads 165°F. Serve immediately.

Variation: Any berry works wonderfully in this dish. Try orange zest instead of or in addition to lemon, too. Enjoy!

Bacon, Corn, and Jalapeño Jack Strata

Ingredients

8 large eggs
3½ cups whole milk
Salt and freshly ground black pepper
1½ cups grated jalapeño jack cheese
¾ lb. loaf French or Italian bread, cut into ½-in. cubes
1 lb. bacon, cut into 1-in. pieces
1 (10-oz.) package frozen corn, thawed and drained
½ cup diced pimiento

Method

Grease the inside of the slow cooker liberally with vegetable oil spray or melted butter. Combine the eggs, milk, salt, and pepper in a mixing bowl, and whisk well. Add cheese and bread cubes, and stir so bread absorbs egg mixture.

Place a large skillet over medium-high heat, and add the bacon pieces. Cook, stirring occasionally, for 5 to 7 minutes or until bacon is crisp. Remove bacon from the pan with a slotted spoon, and add to bread mixture. Stir in corn and pimiento. Transfer mixture to the slow cooker. Cook on low for 4 to 6 hours or until mixture is puffed and an instant-read thermometer inserted in the center reads 165°F. Serve immediately. Enjoy!

Potato, Onion, and Bacon Frittata

Ingredients

½ lb. bacon, cut into 1-in. lengths
2 large red-skinned potatoes, scrubbed and cut into ¼-in. dice
1 large onion, peeled and diced
1 garlic clove, peeled and minced
8 large eggs
¼ cup half-and-half
2 tbsp. chopped fresh parsley
Salt and freshly ground black pepper

Method

Place the bacon in a large skillet over medium-high heat. Cook, stirring occasionally, for 5 to 7 minutes or until bacon is crisp. Remove the bacon from the pan with a slotted spoon and drain on paper towels. Set aside.

Discard all but 3 tbsp. bacon fat from the skillet. Add the potatoes and cook for 10 minutes or until tender, scraping them occasionally with a heavy spatula. Add the onion and garlic to the skillet and cook, stirring frequently, for 5 minutes or until the onion is soft. Whisk the eggs with half-and-half and parsley, and season with salt and pepper. Add vegetable mixture and bacon to eggs.

Grease the inside of the slow cooker liberally with vegetable oil spray or melted butter. Pour the egg mixture into the slow cooker. Cook on high for 2 to 2½ hours or until the eggs are set.

Run a spatula around the sides of the slow cooker and under the bottom of the frittata to release it. Slide it gently onto a serving platter, and cut it into wedges. Serve immediately. Enjoy!

Vegetable Frittata with Pasta

Ingredients

1 (6-oz.) package refrigerated fresh angel-hair pasta
3 tbsp. olive oil
2 small zucchini, rinsed, trimmed, and thinly sliced
4 scallions, trimmed and thinly sliced
3 garlic cloves, peeled and minced
2 ripe plum tomatoes, rinsed, cored, seeded, and finely chopped

3 tbsp. chopped fresh basil or 2 tsp. dried
1 tbsp. chopped fresh oregano or 1 tsp. dried
¼ cup sliced green olives
Salt and freshly ground black pepper
6 large eggs
½ cup freshly grated Parmesan cheese

Method

Cook pasta according to package directions until al dente. Drain and set aside to cool. Then heat olive oil in a large skillet over medium-high heat. Add the zucchini, scallions, and garlic. Cook, stirring frequently, for 5 minutes or until zucchini is tender. Then add the tomatoes, basil, oregano, and olives. Cook mixture, stirring frequently, for 5 minutes or until liquid from tomatoes evaporates. Season with salt and pepper, and cool for 10 minutes.

Grease the inside of the slow cooker liberally with vegetable oil spray or melted butter. Whisk eggs with cheese, and stir in cooked pasta and vegetables. Pour mixture into the slow cooker.

Cook on high for 1½ to 2 hours or until eggs are set. Run a spatula around the sides of the slow cooker and under the bottom of the frittata to release it. Slide it gently onto a serving platter, and cut it into wedges. Serve hot or at room temperature. Enjoy!

Lunch Recipes

Albondigas

Ingredients

½ onion, minced
½ pound ground chuck
¼ cup instant rice, uncooked
2 tbsp. chopped fresh parsley or cilantro
1 egg
Salt and pepper, to taste
4 ounces chopped green chilies --canned, and drained

1 carrot, shredded
4 cups hot water
2 cloves garlic, minced
14 1/2 ounces stewed tomatoes, canned
2 cups low fat beef broth, or water
1 tsp. dried oregano

Method

In a bowl, combine the beef, onion, garlic, rice, egg, salt and pepper to taste. Form into 1 1/2" meatballs. Place chilies and shredded carrots in bottom of slow cooker. Spoon tomatoes evenly on them. Place meatballs on top of the tomatoes. Pour in water, broth, oregano and parsley or cilantro. Cover and cook on LOW 5 1/2 to 6 hours. Garnish this popular Mexican soup with sprigs of fresh cilantro or mint, and serve with flour tortillas. Enjoy!

Alpine Chicken

Ingredients

3/4 tsp. poultry seasoning
2 tbsp. sliced pimento
1 rib celery, thinly sliced,
4 ounces diced Canadian bacon
2 carrots, thinly sliced,
1 tbsp. all-purpose flour
1 (16, oz.) package wide egg noodles, cooked, drained

2 tsp. chicken bouillon granules
1 small onion, thinly sliced
1 tbsp. chopped fresh parsley
¼ cup water
6 Chicken breast halves, boneless skinless
1 (11 oz.,) can condensed cheddar cheese soup,
2 tbsp. grated parmesan cheese

Method

In a small bowl, mix the bouillon granules, chopped parsley, and poultry seasoning. Now keep set aside. Layer the Canadian bacon, carrots, celery and onion in a slow cooker, in order. Add water to the cooker. Remove skin and excess fat from chicken, then rinse and pat dry. Place meat in slow cooker. Sprinkle with half of the reserved seasoning mixture. Top with remaining chicken and sprinkle with remaining seasoning mixture. Stir soup and flour together; spoon over top. DO NOT STIR.

Cover and cook on high for 3 to 3 1/2 hours or on low for 6 to 8 hours or until chicken and vegetables are tender. Spread cooked noodles in a shallow 2 or 2 1/2 quart broiler proof serving dish. Arrange chicken on noodles. Stir the soup mixture and vegetables until combined. Spoon the vegetables over chicken. Sprinkle with pimento and Parmesan cheese. Enjoy!

America's Favorite Pot Roast

Ingredients

3 Carrot, Peeled and sliced
2 tsp. salt
3 ½ Pounds sirloin tip roast, trimmed
1/8 Tsp. tsp., pepper
1/4 Cup water
3 tbsp. flour
3 potatoes, peeled and quartered
2 Small onions, sliced
1 Stalk celery cut in 2" pieces
1/4 Cup flour
1-2 Oz Jar mushrooms, drained or 1/4 Cup mushroom gravy

Method

Trim all excess fat from roast; brown and drain if using chuck or another highly marbled cut. Combine 1/4 cup flour, the salt and pepper. Coat meat with the flour mixture. Place all the vegetables except mushrooms in Crock-Pot and top with roast (cut roast in half, if necessary, to fit easily). Spread mushrooms evenly over top of roast. Cover and cook on Low for 10 to 12 hours. If desired, turn to High during last hour to soften vegetables and make a gravy. Now to thicken the gravy, make a smooth paste of the 3 tbsp. flour and the water and stir into Crock-Pot. Season to taste before serving. Enjoy!

Arizona Chuck Wagon Beans

Ingredients

1 Pound navy beans, Dried Or Pinto
6 Cups Water
1/4 Pound pork loins lean, boneless and, diced
1 Large Onion, chopped
1 garlic clove, minced

1 Large Green pepper, chopped
1 ½ Pounds Round Steak, cubed
1 ½ Teaspoons Salt
½ Tsp. Oregano, crumbled
¼ Tsp. Red pepper
¼ Tsp. Ground cumin

8 Ounces Tomato sauce

Method

Pick over the beans and rinse well. Combine the beans and water in a large kettle. Boil it and cover it, then cook 2 minutes. Remove it from heat and keep aside for 1 hour, and then pour into slow cooker. Add brown salt pork in a large skillet, then remove with a slotted spoon to cooker, now add sauté onion, garlic and green pepper in pan drippings, then remove with slotted spoon to cooker. Add brown beef, a few pieces at a time in pan drippings, now remove from cooker with slotted spoon; stir in salt, oregano, red pepper, cumin and tomato sauce. Add more water, if necessary to bring liquid level above the beans. Cook on low for 10 hours or on high for 6 hours, or until the beans are tender. Enjoy!

Arroz Con Pollo

Ingredients

½ tsp. Salt
¼ tsp. Pepper
1 Clove Garlic, crushed
1 tsp. Oregano
2 tsp. Chili Powder
8 Chicken Thighs Without Skin
½ cup Chicken Broth
2 tbsp. Wine
Red 10 Oz Peas, Frozen, thawed
2 cups Rice, Cooked
2 tbsp. Cilantro, fresh chopped

Method

In a small bowl, combine salt, pepper, garlic, oregano and chili powder. Sprinkle spice mixture over both sides of chicken pieces. Place chicken in slow cooker. Pour broth and wine over chicken. Cover and cook on low 5 to 6 hours. Remove chicken and cover to keep warm. Turn control to high. Add peas. Cover and cook on high 7 to 10 minutes. Stir in cooked rice and chicken until combined. Sprinkle with cilantro and serve. Enjoy!

Asian Spiced Chicken and Beans

Ingredients

½ Cup dry packaged Navy Beans or 1(15 ounces) can Navy Beans, rinsed and drained.
½ Cup dry packaged Red Beans or 1(15 ounce) can Red beans, rinsed and drained.
1 pound boneless skinless chicken breasts, cut into 1/2 inch cubes.
3 large carrots, diagonally sliced
2 to 3 tsp. minced garlic, to taste
2 to 3 tsp. minced ginger root or 1 to 2 tsp. ground ginger, to taste
1 (14 ½ ounces) can reduced-sodium fat-free chicken broth
2 tbsp. cornstarch
½ Tsp. tsp. crushed red pepper
2 to 3 tbsp. reduced sodium soy sauce
4 Cups cooked rice
Sliced green onions and tops, for garnish
Chopped peanuts for garnish

Method

If using dry beans, in a large saucepan, place dry beans and cover with 2 inches water; heat to boiling; let boil, uncovered for 2 to 3 minutes. Remove from heat, cover and set aside for at least 1 hour and up to 4 hours. Drain soaking water and rinse beans. Place soaked OR canned beans, chicken, carrots, garlic, ginger and 1 1/4 cups of the chicken broth in the slow cooker; stir well. Cover and cook on low until beans are tender about 5 1/2 to 6 hours. Turn the slow cooker to high. Combine the cornstarch with the remaining 1/2 cup broth and stir into mixture in cooker; stir in crushed red pepper. Cover and cook until thickened, about 30 minutes. Stir in soy sauce. Serve over rice; sprinkle with green onions and peanuts. Enjoy!

Beef Sandwiches

Ingredients

2 ½ lb. lean boneless chuck roast
¼ cup tomato ketchup
1 tbsp. Dijon-style mustard
2 tbsp. tbsp. brown sugar
1 garlic clove, crushed
1 tbsp. Worcestershire sauce
2 tbsp. tbsp. red wine vinegar
¼ tsp. tsp. liquid smoke flavoring

¼ tsp. tsp. salt
1/8 tsp. tsp. pepper
10 French rolls or sandwich buns (10 to 12)

Method

Place the beef in slow cooker. Combine the remaining ingredients, except rolls. Pour over meat. Cover and cook on LOW 8 to 9 hours. Refrigerate or prepare the sandwiches now. Shred the beef by pulling it apart with 2 forks. Add one cup sauce. Reheat mixture in microwave or on the stove top. Spoon on warm, open-face rolls or buns. Top with additional warm sauce if desired. Enjoy!

Barbecue Beef Sandwiches

Ingredients

3 pounds beef boneless chuck roast
1 cup barbecue sauce
½ cup apricot preserves
2 tbsp.. red or green bell pepper chopped
1 tbsp. Dijon mustard
2 tsp. brown sugar packed
1 small, onion sliced
12 whole hamburger buns or Kaiser rolls split

Method

Remove the excess fat from the beef. Cut the beef into 4 pieces. Place the beef in 4 or 5 quart slow cooker. Mix remaining ingredients except buns and pour the mixture over the beef. Cover and cook on low heat for 7 to 8 hours or until beef is tender. Remove the beef from slow cooker. Cut beef into thin slices and stir it with sauce. Cover and cook on low heat for 20 to 30 minutes longer or until the beef is hot. Fill buns with beef mixture. Spread the buns with horseradish sauce for a delicious flavor kick! Enjoy!

Barbecued Pork

Ingredients

2 lbs. boneless pork top loin
1 cup chopped onion
¾ cup diet soda
¾ cup barbecue sauce

Method

Combine all the ingredients in a crock pot. Cook it covered on high for 5-6 hours or until the meat is very tender. Drain and slice or shred the pork. You can now serve it on wheat buns. Enjoy!

Basil Chicken

Ingredients

4 whole skinless chicken breasts
½ tsp. tsp. pepper
½ tsp. tsp. basil
1 can cream of celery soup
½ whole green pepper,, sliced

Method

Place the chicken breasts in a slow cooker. Sprinkle with pepper and basil. Spread soup on top of the chicken. Arrange slices of green pepper on top of the soup. Cover and cook on low heat for 6 to 8 hours. Enjoy!

Basque-Style Chicken Stew

Ingredients

2 tbsp.. olive oil
6 slices turkey bacon, Louis Rich,, diced ½ inch
8 ounces mushroom,, sliced
1 green bell pepper,, cubed 1"
1 red bell pepper,, cubed 1"
1 bunch green onions,, ½ , 1 "chunks

1 pound boneless skinless chicken breasts,, 1" cubes
2 tbsp.. balsamic vinegar
½ tsp. tsp. marjoram
½ tsp. tsp. salt
¼ tsp. tsp. pepper
¼ cup fat-free chick, broth, 2 cups tomatoes, canned, (16 oz.)

Method

Heat olive oil in a large skillet and sauté the bacon until browned. Add mushrooms, peppers and green onions and sauté for a minute. Add vinegar and cook 1 minute more, scraping up the browned bits from the bottom of the pan. Set it aside. Place the chicken in slow cooker. Add sautéed bacon and vegetable mixture to the pot, and the olives (optional). Combine the remaining ingredients in a bowl and mix. Pour over chicken and vegetables in the slow cooker. Cover and cook on low for 8 to 10 hours. Now you can serve it with rice. Enjoy!

Beef Stew

Ingredients

1 pound beef stew meat,, cubed, 1"
8 tsp. McCormick Beef Stew seasoning,, (1/2 package)
15 ounces green beans, canned, (1 can)
15 ounces canned black beans,, 1 can (shop rite)
15 ounces peas, canned, (1 can)
15 ounces corn, canned, (1 can)
3 cups water

Method

Put all the ingredients in a crock pot and simmer all day (about 8 hours or so). If you cannot find McCormick Beef Stew seasoning use another brand of seasoning or use your own favorite spices i.e. salt, pepper, garlic, or onion soup mix. Enjoy!

Beef Stroganoff

Ingredients

1 ½ lb. beef, trimmed,
1 cup chopped onion
8 oz. sliced mushrooms
1 tbsp. Dijon mustard
2 tsp. dried parsley
½ tsp. salt
½ tsp. dill,, dried
¼ tsp. pepper
1 clove garlic,, minced
½ cup all-purpose flour, 1 can fat-free beef broth, ¾ cup low fat sour cream
6 cups egg noodles, Barilla, cooked

Method

Firstly, trim fat from the steak. Wrap steak in heavy-duty plastic wrap and freeze it for 30 minutes. Unwrap the steak, now cut the steak diagonally across grain into 1/8-inch thick slices. Place the steak, onion, and next 7 ingredients in a 3-quart electric slow cooker. Combine flour and broth in a bowl and stir with a whisk until blended. Add broth mixture to cooker and stir well. Cover the cooker with a lid and cook on low-heat for 8 hours or until tender. Turn off the slow cooker and the remove lid. Let it stand for 10 minutes. Stir in sour cream. Serve stroganoff over noodles. Enjoy!

Bloody Mary Chicken

Ingredients

4 whole boneless, skinless chicken breast
33 ¾ ounces Bloody Mary mix (you can use extra spicy)

Method

Wash the skin and remove fat from chicken breasts and place it in a slow cooker. Pour Bloody Mary mix over the chicken breasts, now put it in a slow cooker and cook it on low heat for 8 hours. Now it's ready to serve. Enjoy!

Burger Heaven Casserole

Ingredients

16 oz. extra lean gr. beef (or turkey)
2 cups sliced raw potatoes
1½ cups sliced carrots (I used frozen)
1 cup chopped celery
½ cup chopped onion
1 cup frozen peas, thawed
1 cup frozen whole kernel corn, thawed
1 10 oz. can healthy Request Tomato Soup
½ cup water
1 tsp. dried parsley flakes
1 can mushrooms
Salt and Pepper

Method

In large skillet mix the brown meat, onion, chopped celery and mushrooms. Now toss it well. Now, in a slow cooker, , spray butter flavored. Combine the meat mixture, potatoes, carrots, peas, and corn. Now, stir in tomato soup, water, parsley flakes and salt and pepper to taste. Cover and cook on low heat 6 to 8 hours. Enjoy!

Slow Cooker Double Onion Beef Sandwiches

Ingredients

3 large cloves garlic, finely chopped
1 tbsp. Worcestershire sauce

½ tsp. coarsely ground pepper

3 lb. fresh beef brisket (not corned beef)

1 medium onion, thinly sliced

1 package (1-3 oz.) onion soup mix

½ cup water

8 individual French rolls or crusty rolls

Method

Mix the garlic, Worcestershire sauce and pepper in a skillet. Now, rub on both sides of beef. Cut the beef into half or thirds to fit slow cooker. Place the sliced onion into bottom of 3 /2-6 quart of slow cooker. Top it with beef pieces and sprinkle it with soup mix (dry). Now, add water and cover and cook on low heat for 8 to 10 hours or until beef is tender. Remove beef and cut across the grain into thin slices. Skim fat from juices in slow cooker. Cut the breads horizontally in half. Fill bread with the beef. Drizzle with juices. Enjoy!

Slow Cooker Enchiladas

Ingredients

1 lb. ground beef (ground turkey)

1 cup chopped onion

½ cup chopped green pepper

1 can kidney beans, rinsed and drained

1 can diced tomatoes w/Green chilies, undrained

1 small can tomato sauce

1 package taco seasoning, dry

1/3 cup water

½ tsp. salt

¼ tsp. pepper

1 cup shredded reduced fat cheese (I used fat free)

6 flour tortillas

Method

In skillet, cook the beef, onion and green pepper until browned. In bowl, add all the other ingredients except tortillas and stir it well. In crock pot layer ¾ beef mixture, then add tortilla. Repeat the same layers with all 6 tortillas. Cover lid, and cook on low heat for 5 to 7 hours. The dish is ready to serve and can be used as a serving for 6. Enjoy!

Slow Cooker Fiesta Tamale Pie

Ingredients

¾ cup yellow cornmeal
1 cup beef broth
1 lb. extra-lean ground beef
1 tsp. chili powder
½ tsp. ground cumin

1 (14 to 16 oz.) jar thick and chunky salsa
1 (16 oz.) can whole-kernel corn, drained
¼ cup sliced ripe olives
2 oz. reduced-fat Cheddar cheese, shredded (1/2 cup)

Method

In a large mixing bowl, mix cornmeal and broth and let stand 5 minutes . Stir in the beef, chili powder, cumin, salsa, corn and olives. Pour into a 3 ½ quart slow cooker. Cover with lid and cook on LOW 5 to 7 hours or until set. Sprinkle cheese over top. Now cover and cook another 5 minutes or until cheese melts. Enjoy!

Slow Cooker Georgia-Style Barbecued Turkey Sandwich

Ingredients

4 turkey thighs (2 ½ to 3 lbs.), skin removed
½ cup firmly packed brown sugar
¼ cup prepared mustard
2 tbsp. Ketchup
2 tbsp. cider vinegar
2 tbsp. Louisiana-style hot pepper sauce

1 tsp. Salt
1 tsp. coarsely ground black pepper
1 tsp. crushed red pepper flakes
2 tsp. liquid smoke
12 sandwich buns, split
½ pint (1 cup) creamy coleslaw (from deli)

Method

Spray 4-6 qt. slow cooker with nonstick cooking spray. Place turkey in spray slow cooker. In small bowl, combine all the remaining ingredients except buns and coleslaw and mix well. Pour over turkey, and keep turning turkey as necessary to coat. Cover and cook on LOW for 8 to 10 hours Remove turkey from slow cooker and place it on large plate. Now remove meat from the bones and discard the bones. Shred the turkey with 2 forks. Now add the turkey to broth and mix well. To serve, with slotted spoon, place about 1/3 cup turkey mixture onto bottom half of each bun. Top each with rounded tbsp. and coleslaw. Cover with top halves of buns. Enjoy!

South-Of-The-Border Lasagna

Ingredients

¾ lb. turkey sausage
2 tomatoes, seeded and chopped
3 fresh tomatillos, husked and chopped
1 (19 oz.) can green enchilada sauce
1 clove garlic, crushed
¼ tsp. Salt
1/8 tsp. ground black pepper
8 oz. lasagna noodles
1 cup low-fat or nonfat ricotta cheese
1 cup shredded reduced-fat jalapeno jack cheese
Chopped fresh cilantro

Method

Crumble the sausages into a slow cooker. Stir in tomatoes, tomatillos, enchilada sauce, garlic, salt, and pepper. Cover and cook on low 5 ½ to 6 hours Preheat oven to 350* Grease a 13 x 9" baking dish. Cook lasagna noodles according to package directions and drain. Spread about ½ cup turkey mixture in bottom of prepared pan. Now arrange alternate layers of noodles, ricotta cheese, and hot turkey mixture in the prepared pan. Top with Jack cheese. Bake 25 to 30 minutes or until bubbly around edges. Sprinkle with cilantro and serve. Enjoy!

Southwestern Bean Stew with Cornmeal Dumplings

Ingredients

1 (15-oz.) can red kidney beans, rinsed and drained
1 15-oz. can black beans, pinto beans, or great northern beans, rinsed and drained
3 cups water
1 (14½-oz.) can Mexican-style stewed tomatoes
1 10-oz. package frozen whole kernel corn, thawed
2 medium carrots, sliced (1 cup)
1 large onion, chopped (1 cup)
1 4-oz. can chopped green chili peppers

2 tsp. instant beef or chicken bouillon granules or 2 vegetable bouillon cubes
1 to 2 tsp. chili powder
2 cloves garlic, minced
1/3 cup all-purpose flour
¼ cup yellow cornmeal
1 tsp. baking powder
Dash salt
Dash pepper
1 beaten egg white
2 tbsp. Milk
1 tbsp. cooking oil

Method

In a 31/2 or 4-quart electric crockery cooker combine canned beans, water, tomatoes, corn, carrots, onion, undrained chili peppers, bouillon granules or cubes, chili powder, and garlic. Cover and cook on low-heat setting for 10 to 12 hours or on high-heat setting for 4 to 5 hours. For dumplings, in a small mixing bowl stir together flour, cornmeal, baking powder, salt, and pepper. In another small mixing bowl combine egg white, milk, and cooking oil. Add egg-white mixture to flour mixture and stir with a fork just until combined. If stew was cooked on low-heat setting, turn crockery cooker to high-heat setting. Drop dumpling mixture in 8 rounded teaspoons atop the stew. Cover and cook for 30 minutes more (do not lift cover). It is ready to serve. Enjoy!

Southwestern Chicken Chili

Ingredients

1 medium green bell pepper, chopped
1 cup chopped onions
3 garlic cloves, minced
3 tbsp.. cornmeal
2 tbsp.. chili powder
3 tsp. dried oregano leaves
1 tsp. tsp. cumin
1 tsp. tsp. salt
1 ¼ Pounds boneless skinless chicken thigh,, cut in 1" pieces
1 Jar 16-Oz. medium picante sauce
1 15-Oz Can pinto beans – undrained
1 14.5-Oz Can Diced Tomatoes – undrained

Method

In a 3½ to 4 quart slow cooker, combine bell pepper, onion and garlic. In a medium bowl, combine corn meal, chili powder, oregano, cumin and salt; mix well. Add chicken and toss it well to coat. Add the chicken and any remaining seasoning mixture to vegetables in the slow cooker. Add picante sauce, beans and tomatoes, now stir gently to mix. Cook on low setting for 6 to 8 hours For a spicy dish, use 3 tbsp. of chili powder. For a less spicy recipe, use mild picante sauce or salsa. Enjoy!

Southwest Meat Loaf

Ingredients
Vegetable cooking spray

2 lbs. ground round (you can use 93% lean ground beef)
3 slices light bread, crumbled (1 cup)
1 cup chopped onion (about 1 medium)
½ cup fat-free egg substitute
¼ tsp. salt
¼ tsp. ground pepper
½ cup ketchup
½ cup thick and chunky salsa (I used chili sauce)

Method

Coat a 3 ½ quart slow cooker with cooking spray. Tear off two lengths of aluminum foil long enough to fit in the bottom of cooker and extend 3 inches over each side of the cooker. Fold each foil strip lengthwise to form 2-inch- wide strips. Arrange foil strips in a cross fashion in the cooker, pressing strip in bottom of the cooker and extending ends over sides of the cooker. Combine beef and next 5 ingredients and shape mixture into a loaf in the shape of the slow cooker container. Place loaf in slow cooker over the foil strips. (Foil strips become "handles" to remove meat loaf from slow cooker.)Make a shallow indention on top of the meat loaf. Combine ketchup and salsa (chili sauce) and then pour it over meat loaf. Cover and cook on low heat 8 hours or on high heat 3½ to 4 hours. Use foil strips to lift meat loaf from cooker. Let meat loaf stand 10 minutes before serving. Enjoy!

Southwestern Slow Cooker Chicken and Potato Soup

Ingredients

¾ LB(s) boneless, skinless chicken breast(s), cut into 1-inch cubes
3 small sweet potatoes, or 2 medium, peeled and cut into 1-inch cubes
1 large onion, chopped
29-oz. can diced tomatoes, salsa-style with chilies, un-drained
14½, oz. fat-free chicken broth
1 tsp. dried oregano
½ tsp. ground cumin
1 ½ cups frozen corn kernels, not thawed

Method

Mix the chicken, potatoes, onion, tomatoes, broth, oregano and cumin in a 4- quart or larger slow cooker (crock pot) and cover it. Now cook on low heat setting for at least 6 hours. Stir in the corn. Now cover and cook on high heat setting until chicken is no longer pink in the center and vegetables are tender, about 30 minutes. Enjoy!

Special Chicken Cacciatore

Ingredients

1 cup (1 8-ounce can) tomatoes, finely chopped and undrained
1 (10 ¾ -ounce) can Healthy Request Tomato Soup
1 ½ tsp. Italian seasoning
½ tsp. tsp. dried minced garlic
½ cup (one 2.5-ounce jar) sliced mushrooms, drained
½ cup chopped green bell pepper
½ cup chopped onion
16 ounces skinned and boned uncooked chicken breast, cut into 4 pieces

Method

In a slow cooker container sprayed with olive oil-flavored cooking spray, combine the undrained tomatoes, tomato soup, Italian seasoning, and garlic. Mix it well. Now stir in mushrooms, green pepper, and onion. Add the chicken pieces. Mix well to combine and coat. Cover and cook on LOW for 6 to 8 hours. When serving, evenly spoon sauce over the chicken. Enjoy!

Spicy Wine Pot Roast

Ingredients

3 pounds beef pot roast
1 small onion, chopped
1 package brown gravy mix
1 cup water
¼ cup ketchup
¼ cup dry red wine
2 tsp. Dijon-style mustard

1 tsp. tsp. Worcestershire sauce
1/8 tsp. tsp. garlic powder
½ tsp. tsp. dried Italian seasoning
Salt
Freshly ground black pepper
Fresh parsley, for garnish,, chopped

Method

Firstly, sprinkle the meat with salt and pepper. Place it in crock pot. Combine the remaining ingredients, except parsley, and pour over the meat. Cover and cook on low for 10 hours. Remove the meat and slice. Thicken sauce with flour mixed in a small amount of water and serve over meat sprinkled with chopped parsley. Enjoy!

Stir-Fry Lo Mein

Ingredients

2 tbsp. Butter
1 (20-oz.) boneless skinless chicken thigh, cut into bite-size pieces.
1 cup stir-fry seasoning sauce
1 (5-oz.) can water chestnuts, drained
1 medium onion, sliced
1 (16-oz.) package fresh stir-fry vegetables (celery, carrots, broccoli and pea pods)
½ cup whole cashews (optional)
1 (8-oz.) package. lo mien noodles

Method

Melt butter in 10" skillet until sizzling and add the chicken pieces to the skillet. Cook over medium, high heat, turning occasionally, until chicken is browned (5 to 7 minutes). Place in slow cooker. Add stir-fry seasoning sauce, water chestnuts and onion. Cover and cook on LOW heat setting for 4-6 hours. Increase heat setting to HIGH 30 minutes before serving. Add stir-fry vegetables and stir. Cover and cook 30 minutes, stirring once, until vegetables are crispy and tender. Stir in cashews just before serving, if desired. Meanwhile, cook lo mien noodles according to package directions. To serve, spoon stir-fry chicken and vegetables mixture over noodles. This can be made with frozen stir-fry vegetables. Increase the heat setting to HIGH and cook for 45 minutes to 1 hour until vegetables are tender. Enjoy!

Stuffed Beef Rolls

Ingredients

1 ½ lbs. Top Round Steak,, ½" inch thick.
4 slices reduced fat bacon
¾ cup celery,, diced
¾ cup onion,, diced
½ cup green bell pepper,, diced
10 ounces Beef gravy
Garlic powder to taste,

Method

Cut the steak into four equal size pieces. Now sprinkle garlic powder on the steak pieces. Place one bacon slice on each piece of meat. Mix celery, onion and green pepper in medium bowl and place about ½ cup of mixture on each piece of meat. Roll up meat and secure ends with wooden toothpicks. Now set the meat on a paper towel to absorb any extra meat juice. Place steak rolls in crock-pot. Pour gravy evenly over steak rolls to thoroughly moisten. Cover crock-pot and cook on Low 8 to 10 hours or High 4 to 5 hours. Skim off any fat before serving. Enjoy!

Stuffed Pasta Shells with Mushroom Sauce

Ingredients

8 oz. mushrooms, sliced
2 tsp. olive oil
2 soy-sausage patties (or regular breakfast sausage)
1 can (28 oz.) plum tomatoes, cut-up
1 can (6 oz.) low-sodium tomato paste
½ tsp. dried oregano
½ tsp. garlic powder
½ cup dry white wine
1 package (20 oz.) low-fat cheese stuffed pasta shells
Snipped fresh Italian parsley, for garnish

Method

Sauté the mushrooms in oil in a nonstick skillet, until golden or about 5 minutes. Transfer them to the crockery pot. In the same skillet, cook the sausage patties for 6 minutes. Remove them from the skillet, and cut them into 1/4" cubes. Place the pieces in the crockery pot. Stir in the tomatoes, tomato paste, oregano, garlic, and wine. Cover and cook on high for 3 ½ to 5 hrs. Add the shells to the sauce, making certain to cover them with sauce. Cover and cook until the shells are thoroughly hot, about 1 hour. Garnish with the parsley. Enjoy!

Sunday Italian Vegetable Soup

Ingredients

½ cup Dry navy beans
Water
4 cups Chicken broth
¾ cup Carrot, sliced, peeled
½ cup Potato, sliced with peel
1 tbsp. Corn oil
½ cup Onion,, sliced
2 cups canned Italian tomatoes,, undrained

2 cups Cabbage,, sliced thinly
1 cup Zucchini,, sliced
½ cup Celery,, sliced
½ cup canned chickpeas, (garbanzo beans), drained canned
½ cup Rotini or other pasta,, uncooked
1 tbsp. fresh parsley,, finely minced fresh
2 tsp. Dried basil,, crumbled
¼ tsp. tsp. Salt

¼ tsp. tsp. Ground pepper,

Method

Cover navy beans with water in a large pot. Cook over medium heat, bring it just to the boiling point. Remove pan from heat, cover, and let stand for 1 hour. Drain the water from the pot. Add the chicken broth, carrot, and potato. Cover and cook over medium heat until vegetables are almost tender, about 35 minutes. Heat oil in a small skillet and sauté onion until tender. Add onion and all remaining ingredients to soup pot. Cook 15 minutes or until pasta is cooked. Serve hot. Enjoy!

Supper Pot Potluck

Ingredients

16 ounces ground 90% lean turkey or beef
3 cups (15 ounces) sliced raw potatoes
11/2 cups chopped celery
2 cups sliced carrots
1 cup chopped onion
1-1/2 cups frozen peas
2 tsp. Italian seasoning
1-3/4 cups (one 15 ounce can) Hunt's Chunky Tomato Sauce

Method

In a large skillet sprayed with butter-flavored cooking spray, add the brown meat. Meanwhile place potatoes, celery, carrots, and onion in Crock-Pot container. Sprinkle peas over top. Spoon browned meat over vegetables. Stir Italian seasoning into tomato sauce. Evenly pour sauce over meat. Cover and cook on LOW 6 to 8 hours. Stir well just before serving. Enjoy!

Sweet and Sour Wings

Ingredients

3 pounds chicken wings, (about 28 wings pieces) or 18 drum sticks
1 cup packed brown sugar
¼ cup all-purpose flour
½ cup water
¼ cup white vinegar
1 ½ tbsp. ketchup
¼ cup soy sauce

¼ tsp. garlic powder
1 tbsp. onion flakes
½ tsp. tsp. salt
½ tsp. tsp. prepared mustard

Method

Discard tip and cut wings apart at joint. Place the chicken pieces in 5 quart slow cooker. Mix brown sugar and flour well in saucepan. Add water, vinegar and ketchup and stir well. Now add remaining 5 ingredients. Heat and stir until boiling and thickened. Pour the mixture over wings. Now cover and Cook on LOW for 8 to 9 hours or on HIGH for 4 to 41/2 hours until tender. Serve from slow cooker or remover to platter. Enjoy!

Sweet and Sour Meat and Rice

Ingredients

16 oz. extra lean ground turkey or beef
1 cup crushed pineapple, packed in fruit juice, undrained
1 ¾ cups tomato sauce
2 tbsp. brown sugar twin
1 tbsp. reduced sodium soy sauce
1 ½ cups chopped green pepper
1 cup chopped onion
2 tsp. dried parsley flakes
1 1/3 cups uncooked instant rice

Method

In a large skillet sprayed with butter-flavored cooking spray, add the brown meat. Spray a slow cooker container with butter-flavored spray. Now in the prepared container, combine undrained pineapple, tomato sauce, brown sugar, and soy sauce. Mix it well. Stir in green pepper, onion, and parsley flakes. Add browned meat and uncooked rice. Mix well to combine. Cover and cook on low for 6 hours. Mix well before serving. Enjoy!

Sweet & Spicy "DUMP" Chicken

Ingredients

1 Package Taco Seasoning Mix
8 oz. Apricot Jam

12 oz. Salsa
1 ½ Pounds Chicken Pieces

Method

Put chicken in the bottom of the pot, pour over the remaining ingredients (mixed) and cook until the chicken is done. This should take about 3 to 4 hours. Enjoy!

Swiss Chicken Casserole

Ingredients

1 package of stove top stuffing mix
4-6 boneless, skinless chicken breasts
4 slices of Swiss cheese
1 can of reduced fat cream of mushroom soup

Ingredients

Take 1 package of stove top stuffing mix and mix both dry packets together. Do not add water yet. Place in a sprayed (with Pam) crock pot. Place the 4-6 boneless, skinless chicken breasts on top of the stuffing. Place the Swiss cheese on top of the chicken and then spread the reduced fat cream of mushroom soup on top of the chicken and cheese. Drizzle 1/2 cup of warm water around the edges of the cooker. Cook on low in crock pot all day. Enjoy!

Swiss Steak

Ingredients

1 ½ lb. beef top round steak (1/2" thick), cut into serving-size pcs.
2 cups sliced onions
1 (4.5 oz.) jar whole mushrooms, drained
1 (10 3/4 oz.) can condensed beef broth
¼ tsp. Salt
¼ tsp. Pepper
¼ cup water
2 tbsp. Cornstarch

Method

Firstly, pre-heat oven to 325 F. In large ovenproof skillet, Dutch oven or baking dish, combine all ingredients except water and cornstarch and mix well. Now cover and Bake at 325F for 2 ½-3 hours or until beef is tender. In small bowl, combine water and cornstarch, and then, stir into beef mixture. Bake an additional 15 minutes or until gravy has thickened. Enjoy!

Swiss Steak #2

Ingredients

1 ½ lb. beef boneless round steak, about 3/4" thick
½ tsp. prepared seasoned salt
6 to 8 new potatoes, cut into fourths
1 ½ cups baby-cut carrots
1 medium onion, sliced
1 can (14 1/2 oz.) diced tomatoes with basil, garlic and oregano, undrained
1 jar (12 oz.) home-style beef gravy
Chopped fresh parsley, if desired

Method

Remove excess fat from the beef. Cut beef into 6 serving pieces. Spray 12" skillet with cooking spray and heat over medium-high heat. Sprinkle the beef with seasoned salt. Cook beef in skillet for about 8 minutes, turning once, until brown. Now layer potatoes, carrots, beef and onion in a 3 1/2 to 6 quart slow cooker. Mix tomatoes and gravy, now spoon the mixture over beef and vegetables. Cover and cook on LOW 7-9 hours or until beef and vegetables are tender. Sprinkle with parsley. Enjoy!

Tarragon-Mustard Turkey with Fettuccine

Ingredients

1 lb. boneless, skinless turkey breast
2 leeks
2 stalks celery, chopped
1 tbsp. chopped fresh tarragon
2 tbsp. Dijon mustard
1 tbsp. fresh lemon juice
1 tbsp. brown sugar

1 tsp. instant chicken bouillon granules
¼ tsp. Salt
1/8 tsp. ground black pepper
2 tbsp. Cornstarch
2 tbsp. cold water
6 to 8 oz. fettuccine or medium pasta shells

Method

Cut turkey into thin strips, about 1 x 1/4". Trim leeks and halve lengthwise. Rinse and slice. Combine turkey and leeks in a 3 1/2 quart slow cooker with celery. In a small bowl, combine the tarragon, lemon juice, mustard, brown sugar, bouillon granules, salt, and pepper. Mix it well, now spoon it over turkey. Cover and cook on LOW 4 ½ to 5 hours or until turkey and vegetables are tender. Turn control to HIGH. Dissolve cornstarch in a small bowl. Stir into cooking juices in slow cooker. Cover and cook on HIGH 20-30 minutes or until thickened. Cook pasta according to package directions and drain. Spoon the turkey mixture over cooked pasta. Serve hot. Enjoy!

Teriyaki Steak

Ingredients

1 LB Flank Steak
¼ cup Soy Sauce
1 cup Pineapple Chunks in Juice – Drained, 1/4 cup juice reserved
1 tsp. Ginger Root – grated
1 tbsp. Sugar
1 tbsp. oil
2 Clove Garlic, crushed
3 tbsp. Cornstarch
3 tbsp. Water

Method

Cut the meat into 1/8-inch slices and place in a slow cooker. In a small bowl, combine soy sauce, reserved pineapple juice, gingerroot, sugar oil and garlic. Pour sauce mixture over meat. Cover and cook on LOW for 6 to 7 hours. Turn heat to HIGH. Stir in the pineapple. Combine cornstarch and water in a small bowl; add to cooker. Cook, keep stirring, until slightly thickened. Serve over rice. Enjoy!

Texas Chili

Ingredients

1 ½ lb. beef top round steak, trimmed, cut into 3/4" cubes
1 small onion, finely chopped
2 garlic cloves, minced
1 (28 oz.) can diced tomatoes, undrained
1 (8 oz.) can tomato sauce
1 (15.5 oz. or 16 oz.) can pinto beans, undrained
1 (4.5 oz.) can chopped green chilies
3 tsp. chili powder
1 tsp. Cumin
Toppings:
Sour cream, Shredded Cheddar cheese, Sliced green onions

Method

Combine all the ingredients in the slow cooker and cook on low for 10 to 12 hours or until the beef is done. Serve hot, Enjoy!

Tex-Mex Bean Stew with Cornmeal Dumplings

Ingredients

1 15-oz. can red kidney beans, rinsed and drained
1 15-oz. can black beans rinsed and drained
3 cups water
1 14 ½-oz. can Mexican-style stewed tomatoes
1 10-oz. package frozen whole kernel corn, thawed
2 medium carrots, sliced (1 cup)
1 cup large onion, chopped (1 cup)
1 4-oz. can chopped green chili peppers

2 tsp. chicken bouillon granules
1 to 2 tsp. chili powder
2 cloves garlic, minced
1/3 cup all-purpose flour
¼ cup yellow cornmeal
1 tsp. baking powder
Dash salt
Dash pepper
1 beaten egg white
2 tbsp. Milk
1 Tbsp. cooking oil

Method

In a 31/2- or 4-quart electric crockery cooker combine canned beans, water, tomatoes, corn, carrots, onion, undrained chili peppers, bouillon granules, chili powder, and garlic. Cover and cook on low-heat setting for 10 to 12 hours or on high-heat setting for 4 to 5 hours. For dumplings, in a small mixing bowl stir together flour, cornmeal, baking powder, salt, and pepper. In another small mixing bowl combine egg white, milk, and cooking oil. Add egg-white mixture to flour mixture and stir with a fork just till combined. If stew was cooked on low-heat setting, turn crockery cooker to high-heat setting. Drop dumpling mixture in 8 rounded teaspoons atop the stew. Cover and cook for 30 minutes more (do not lift cover). Enjoy!

Tex-Mex Chicken 'N' Rice

Ingredients

2 cups converted rice, uncooked; Uncle Ben's
28 ounces diced tomatoes, Hunt's
6 ounces tomato paste
3 cups hot water
1 package taco seasoning mix

1 pound boneless & skinless chicken breast, cut in 1/2" cubes
2 medium onions,, cho9pped
1 medium green bell pepper,, chopped
4 ounces green chilies,, diced
¾ tsp. tsp. garlic pepper

Method

In a slow cooker mix together all the ingredients except chilies and garlic pepper. Cover and cook on low heat for 4 to 4 ½ hours or until the rice is tender and the chicken is white throughout (do not overcook or the rice will be mushy). Stir in the chilies and garlic pepper. Serve at once. Enjoy!

Tex-Mex Turkey Wraps (Makes 16 wraps)

Ingredients

2 lbs. turkey breast tenderloins
¼ tsp. seasoned salt
¼ tsp. pepper
1 medium onion, chopped (1/2 cup)
1/3 cup water
2 envelopes (1 1/4 oz. each) taco seasoning mix
16 flour tortillas (8-10" in diameter)
2 cups bite-size pieces lettuce
2 cups shredded Cheddar cheese (8 oz.)

Method

Place turkey in a 3 1/2-4 quart. Slow cooker. Sprinkle with seasoned salt and pepper. Add onion and water to the cooker. Now cover and cook on LOW 6-7 hours or until juice of turkey is no longer pink when centers of thickest pieces are cut. Remove turkey from slow cooker. Shred turkey, using 2 forks. Measure liquid from slow cooker; add enough water to liquid to measure 2 cups. Mix seasoning mixes (dry) and liquid mixture in slow cooker. Stir in shredded turkey. Now cover and cook on LOW for 1 hour. Spoon about 1/4 cup turkey onto center of each tortilla then top it with lettuce and cheese. Roll up tortillas. Ready to serve. Enjoy!

Three Pepper Steak

Ingredients

1 (1 to 1 ¼ lb.) beef flank steak

1 yellow bell pepper
1 green bell pepper
¼ tsp. Salt
½ tsp. red pepper flakes
3 green onions, including some tops, chopped
2 tbsp. soy sauce
2 medium tomatoes, chopped

Method

Trim all visible fat from the steak. Place the steak in a 3 1/2 quart slow cooker. Remove stems and seeds from yellow and green bell peppers and cut them into strips. Arrange bell peppers on the steak. Sprinkle with salt. Top with red pepper flakes, green onions, soy sauce, and tomatoes. Cover and cook on LOW 6 to 7 hours or until steak is tender. Enjoy!

Tomato-Tortilla Soup

Ingredients

4 cups crushed tomatoes
1 ¼ cups vegetable broth
2 medium onions, finely chopped
3 cloves garlic, minced
2 dried cayenne peppers, minced, or 2 tsp. crushed red pepper flakes
1 tbsp. dried parsley
6 corn tortillas, cut into 3/4" strips
1 cup (4 oz.) shredded Monterrey Jack cheese

Method

Combine the first 6 ingredients in the slow cooker. Cover and cook on LOW 7 to 9 hours or on HIGH 3 ½ to 5 hours. Place the tortillas on the baking sheet, and mix them with the olive oil spray. Boil them until they're crisp and golden, about 5 min. Divide the soup among 6 bowls, and top each serving with tortilla strips and cheese. Enjoy!

Touch of the Orient Chicken

Ingredients

6 whole chicken legs , (not leg quarters)
½ cup soy sauce

¼ cup light brown sugar
2 cloves garlic,, minced
1 8 oz. can tomato sauce

Method

Remove skin from the chicken. Use a paper towel to make this slippery task easier. Now place the chicken in a slow cooker. In a medium bowl combine soy sauce, brown sugar, garlic, and tomato sauce and stir well. Pour sauce over the chicken. Cover and cook on low about 6 to 8 hours or until chicken is tender. Serve with rice. Enjoy!

Tuna Noodle Casserole

Ingredients

2 Cans cream of celery soup
1/3 Cup dry sherry
2/3 Cup skim milk
2 tbsp. parsley flakes
10 Ounces frozen peas
2 Cans tuna,, drained
10 Ounces egg noodles,, cooked (no yolk)
2 tbsp. light margarine
1 Dash curry powder, (optional)

Method

In a large bowl, thoroughly combine soup, sherry, milk, parsley flakes, vegetables, and tuna. Fold in noodles. Pour into greased crock-pot. Dot with butter or margarine. Cover and cook on Low 7 to 9 hours. (Cook noodles just until tender.) Enjoy!

Turkey Crock Casserole

Ingredients

1 ½ cups diced cooked turkey breast (8 ounces)
10 slices reduced-calorie bread, made into soft crumbs
¾ cup celery
¼ cup chopped onion
2 cups Campbell's Healthy Request chicken broth (16-ounce can)
3 tbsp.. all-purpose flour
½ tsp. tsp. Poultry Seasoning
¼ tsp. tsp. black pepper

1 tsp. tsp. dried parsley flakes

Method

In a slow cooker container, combine the turkey, bread crumbs, celery and onion. In a covered jar, combine the chicken broth and flour. Shake well. Pour the mixture into a medium saucepan sprayed with butter-flavored cooking spray. Cook over medium heat, stirring often, until mixture thickens. Stir in Poultry Seasoning, black pepper and parsley flakes. Pour broth mixture over turkey mixture. Mix well to combine. Cover and cook on low 6 to 8 hours. Serves 4. Enjoy!

Turkey-Tomato Soup

Ingredients

1 pound turkey thighs, boned, skinned,, cut into 1" pieces (2 medium)
2 small red potatoes,, cubed (or white)
1 ¾ cups fat-free reduced-sodium chicken broth
1 ½ cups frozen corn
1 cup chopped onion
1 cup water

8 ounces no salt added tomato sauce, (1 can)
¼ cup tomato paste
2 tbsp.. Dijon mustard
1 tsp. tsp. hot pepper sauce
½ tsp. tsp. sugar
½ tsp. tsp. garlic powder
¼ cup finely chopped fresh parsley

Method

Combine all ingredients, except parsley, in slow cooker. Cover and cook on LOW 9 to 10 hours. Stir in parsley and serve. Enjoy!

Tuscan Pasta

Ingredients

1 pound boneless skinless chicken breasts, cut into 1 inch
1 can (15 1/2 ounces) red kidney beans, rinsed & drained
1 can (15 oz. each) Italian-style stewed tomatoes
1 jar (4 1/2 oz.) sliced mushrooms, drained
1 medium green bell pepper, chopped
½ cup onion, chopped
½ cup celery, chopped
4 cloves garlic, minced
1 cup water
1 tsp. dried Italian seasoning

6 oz. thin spaghetti, broken into halves

Method

Place all ingredients except spaghetti in slow cooker. Cover and cook on LOW for 4 hours or until veggies are tender. Turn to HIGH. Stir in spaghetti and cover. Stir again after 10 minutes. Cover and cook 45 minutes or until pasta is tender. Garnish with basil and bell pepper strips, if desired. Enjoy!

Vegetable Medley

Ingredients

4 Cups diced peeled potatoes
1 ½ cups frozen whole kernel corn
4 medium tomatoes, seeded and diced
1 cup sliced carrots
½ chopped onion
¾ Tsp. tsp. Salt
½ Tsp. tsp. Sugar
½ Tsp. tsp. Dill weed
1/8 Tsp. tsp. pepper

Method

Combine all ingredients in a slow cooker. Cover and cook on low for 5 to 6 hours or until vegetables are tender. Enjoy!

Vegetarian Navy Bean Soup

Ingredients

16 ounces navy beans, rinsed
8 cups water
1 cup carrots,, finely chopped
1 cup celery,, finely chopped & leaves
½ cup onion,, finely chopped
1 cup tomato vegetable cocktail juice
1 tbsp. chicken-flavor instant bouillon
1/8 tsp. tsp. crushed red pepper flakes

Method

In large saucepan or Dutch oven, combine the beans and water. Boil it for 30 minutes. Let stand 1-1/2 hours or until beans are tender. In slow cooker, combine the beans (and water) and all remaining ingredients and mix well. Cover and cook on low setting for 6 to 8 hours or until beans and vegetables are very tender. Enjoy!

White Bean and Green Chile Pepper Soup

Ingredients

30 ounces great northern beans, canned, (2, 15 oz. cans) rinsed and drained
1 cup finely chopped yellow onion
4 ½ ounces diced green chilies, (1 can)
1 tsp. tsp. ground cumin – divided
½ tsp. tsp. garlic powder
14 ½ ounces fat-free chicken broth, (1 can)
¼ cup chopped fresh cilantro leaves
1 tbsp. extra-virgin olive oil
1/3 cup sour cream

Method

Combine the beans, onion, chilies, 1/2 tsp. cumin and garlic powder in slow cooker. Cook on LOW 8 hours or on HIGH 4 hours. Stir in cilantro, olive oil and remaining 1/2 tsp. cumin. Garnish with sour cream, if desired. Makes 5 servings. Enjoy!

White Chili

Ingredients

1 pound dry great northern beans, rinsed and sorted
4 cups chicken broth
2 cups chopped onions
3 garlic cloves, minced
2 tsp. ground cumin
1 ½ teaspoons dried oregano

1 tsp. tsp. ground coriander
1/8 tsp. tsp. ground cloves
1/8 tsp. tsp. cayenne pepper
1 can (4-oz) chopped green chilies
½ pound boneless skinless chicken breasts, grilled and cubed
1 tsp. salt

Method

Place the beans in a soup kettle or Dutch oven and add water to cover by 2 inches. Bring to a boil for 2 minutes. Remove from heat and cover it now let stand 1 hour. Drain and rinse beans, discarding liquid. Place the beans in a slow cooker. Add the broth, onions, garlic, and seasonings. Cover and cook on low for 7-8 hours or until beans are almost tender. Add the chilies, chicken and salt, now cover and cook for 1 hour or until the beans are tender. Serve with cheese (if desired – must add the points!) Enjoy!

Wiener Bean Pot

Ingredients

20 ounces (2 16 oz. cans) great northern beans rinsed and drained
1 3/4 cups (one 15 oz. can) Hunts Tomato Sauce
2 tbsp. Brown Sugar Twin
l tbsp. prepared mustard
l tsp. dried parsley flakes
12 oz. Healthy Choice 97% fat free frankfurters diced
½ cup chopped onion

Method

In a slow cooker container, combine great northern beans, tomato sauce, brown sugar twin, mustard, and parsley flakes. Add the frankfurters and onion. Mix well to combine. Cover and cook on LOW for 6 to 8 hours. Mix well before serving. Enjoy!

Easy Mexican Corn and Bean Soup

Ingredients

2 ½ cups tomato juice
1 can (14 ½ ounces) diced tomatoes, undrained, puréed
2 cups whole kernel corn
2 cups canned kidney beans
¾ cup finely chopped large onion
¾ cup green bell pepper
1 clove garlic, minced
1 tbsp. chili powder
1 tsp. tsp. ground cumin
1 tsp. sugar
Salt and pepper, to taste

Method

Combine all ingredients, except salt and pepper, in slow cooker. Now cover and cook on high 3 to 4 hours. Season to taste with salt and pepper. Enjoy!

Black Magic Garlic Chowder

Ingredients

4 first-course servings
1 can (15 ounces) black beans, rinsed, drained, divided
1 can (14 ounces) reduced-sodium vegetable broth, divided
1 garlic bulb, cloves peeled, thinly sliced or chopped
2 small serrano chilies, seeded, minced
1 pound plum tomatoes, coarsely chopped
Salt and pepper, to taste
Chili Croutons (recipe on this book)
¼ cup chopped parsley
¼ cup reduced-fat sour cream

Method

Process 3/4 cup beans and 3/4 cup broth in food processor or blender until smooth. Combine puréed and whole black beans with the remaining broth, garlic, chilies, and tomatoes in slow cooker. Now cover and cook on low heat for 6 to 8 hours. Season to taste with salt and pepper. Top each bowl of chowder with Chili Croutons, parsley, and a dollop of sour cream. Enjoy!

Chili Croutons

Ingredients

1 ½ cups cubed firm or day-old French bread (1/2-inch)
Vegetable cooking spray
1 tbsp. Chili powder

Method

Spray bread cubes with cooking spray and sprinkle lightly with chili powder and toss. Arrange in single layer in baking pan and bake at 375 degrees F until browned, 8 to 10 minutes, stirring occasionally. Enjoy!

Garlic Vegetable Soup

Ingredients

2 quarts water
1 can (15 ounces) navy or Great Northern beans, rinsed, drained

1 pound tomatoes, peeled, seeded, coarsely chopped
1 cup each: diced new potatoes, coarsely chopped carrots, cut green beans (1/2-inch), chopped leeks (white parts only)
½ cup chopped celery
6 large cloves garlic, minced
2 tbsp.. tomato paste
2 tbsp. dried basil leaves
Salt and pepper, to taste

Method

Combine all the ingredients, except salt and pepper, in 6 quart slow cooker. Now cover and cook on low heat for 6 to 8 hours. Now for seasoning add salt and pepper to taste. Enjoy!

Savory Mushroom and Barley Soup

Ingredients

3 cups water
1 can (14 ½ ounces) diced tomatoes, undrained
¾ cup chopped onion
¾ cup celery
¾ cup carrots
1 tsp. tsp. dried savory leaves
¾ tsp. tsp. crushed fennel seeds
2 cups sliced crimini or white mushrooms
½ cup quick-cooking barley
Salt and pepper, to taste

Method

Combine all the ingredients, except barley, salt, and pepper, in slow cooker, Now cook on high heat for 4 to 6 hours. Add barley during last 30 minutes. For seasoning add salt and pepper to taste. Enjoy!

Shiitake-Portobello Chowder

Ingredients

3 cups reduced-sodium vegetable broth
4 shallots, thinly sliced
2 large potatoes, cubed (1/4-inch)

2 cups each: sliced shiitake mushroom caps, cubed Portobello mushrooms
2 tbsp.. Marsala wine (optional)
Salt and white pepper, to taste
¼ cup (1 ounce) shredded Gruyère or Swiss cheese

Method

Combine all the ingredients, except wine, salt, white pepper, and cheese, in slow cooker Now cover and cook on high heat for 4 to 5 hours. Stir in wine and season to taste with salt and white pepper. Sprinkle each bowl of soup with cheese. Enjoy!

Sweet Red Pepper Soup

Ingredients

Use jarred roasted peppers for this soup, or roast 3 medium red bell peppers.
1 can (14 ½ ounces) vegetable broth
1 jar (15 ounces) roasted red bell peppers, drained
1 cup tomato juice
1 medium onion, chopped
½ small jalapeño chili, seeded, minced
1 clove garlic, minced
½ tsp. tsp. dried marjoram leaves
Salt and pepper, to taste
¼ – ½ cup reduced-fat sour cream
Sliced green onions, as garnish

Method

Combine all the ingredients, except salt, pepper, sour cream, and green onions, in slow cooker. Now cover and cook on high heat for 2 to 3 hours. Now process soup in food processor or blender. For seasoning add salt and pepper to taste. Serve warm or refrigerate and serve chilled. Top each bowl of soup with a dollop of sour cream and sprinkle with green onions. Enjoy!

Any-Season Vegetable Stew

Ingredients

1 ½ cups reduced-sodium vegetable broth, divided
2 medium tomatoes, chopped
8 ounces green beans
8 ounces small new potatoes, halved

2 sliced small carrots

2 turnips

4 green onions, sliced

½ tsp. tsp. dried marjoram leaves

¼ tsp. tsp. dried thyme leaves

4 slices vegetarian bacon, fried crisp, crumbled

1 cup frozen thawed peas

1 cup artichoke hearts

8 asparagus spears, cut (2-inch)

2 tbsp.. cornstarch

¼ cup cold water

Salt and pepper, to taste

3 cups cooked rice, warm

Method

Combine all the ingredients, except vegetarian bacon, peas, artichoke hearts, asparagus, cornstarch, water, salt, pepper, and rice, in slow cooker. Now cover and cook on high heat for 3 to 4 hours. Now add the bacon, peas, artichoke hearts, and asparagus during last 30 minutes. Stir in combined cornstarch and water, keep stirring for 2 to 3 minutes. For seasoning add salt and pepper to taste, and serve over rice. Enjoy!

Veggie Stew with Chili-Cheese Biscuits

Ingredients

2 cans (14 ½ ounces each) diced tomatoes, undrained

1 can (15 ounces) each: black-eyed peas and red beans, rinsed, drained

2 cups chopped onions

1 ½ cups peeled cubed butternut or acorn squash

1 cup coarsely chopped poblano chilies

1 cup red and yellow bell peppers

3 cloves garlic, minced

2–3 tbsp.. chili powder

1 ½ 2 tsp. ground cumin

¾ tsp. tsp. dried oregano

¾ tsp. marjoram leaves

1 cup fresh or frozen thawed okra

Salt and pepper, to taste

3 large buttermilk biscuits, baked, halved

Chili powder

1/2 cup (2 ounces) shredded reduced-fat Cheddar cheese

Method

Combine all the ingredients, except okra, salt, pepper, biscuits, chili powder, and cheese, in 6-quart slow cooker. Now cover and cook on low heat for 6 to 8 hours, adding okra during last 30 minutes. For seasoning add salt and pepper to taste. Place the biscuits, cut sides down, on stew; sprinkle with chili powder and cheese. Cover and cook until cheese is melted, about 5 minutes. Enjoy!

Vegetable Garden Stew

Ingredients

2 cups vegetable broth
8 ounces sliced mushrooms
8 ounces cauliflower florets
8 ounces cubed potatoes
2 medium onions
2 tomatoes, cut into wedges
2 cloves garlic, minced
1 tsp. tsp. dried savory leaves
1 bay leaf
2 small zucchini, sliced
Salt and pepper, to taste
3 cups cooked millet or couscous, warm

Method

Combine all the ingredients, except zucchini, salt, pepper, and millet, in slow cooker. Now cover and cook on low heat for 6 to 8 hours, adding zucchini during last 30 minutes. For seasoning add salt and pepper to taste. Discard bay leaf and serve over millet in shallow bowls. Enjoy!

Sweet-Sour Squash and Potato Stew

Ingredients

1 can (14 ½ ounces) diced tomatoes, undrained
1 cup apple cider or apple juice
3 cups peeled cubed butternut or acorn squash
3 cups Idaho potatoes
2 cups peeled cubed sweet potatoes
2 cups sliced unpeeled tart green apples
1 ½ cups whole-kernel corn
½ cup chopped shallots
½ cup red bell pepper
2 cloves garlic, minced
1 ½ tbsp.. honey
1 ½ tbsp. cider vinegar

1 bay leaf
¼ tsp. tsp. ground nutmeg
2 tbsp.. cornstarch
¼ cup cold water
Salt and pepper, to taste
4 cups cooked basmati or jasmine rice, warm

Method

Combine all the ingredients, except cornstarch, water, salt, pepper, and rice, in 6-quart slow cooker. Now cover and cook on low heat for 6 to 8 hours. Turn heat to high and cook 10 minutes, then stir in combined cornstarch and water, and keep stirring 2 to 3 minutes. Discard bay leaf, for seasoning add salt and pepper to taste. Serve over rice. Enjoy!

Wild Mushroom Stew

Ingredients

3 cans (15 ounces each) Great Northern beans, rinsed, drained
1 cup reduced-sodium vegetable broth
½ cup dry white wine or vegetable broth
2 cups chopped Portobello mushrooms
2 cups sliced shiitake
2 cups crimini
2 cups white mushrooms
1 cup sliced leeks (white parts only)
1 cup chopped red bell pepper
½ cup chopped onion
1 tbsp. minced garlic
½ tsp. tsp. dried rosemary
½ tsp. thyme leaves
1/8–1/4 tsp. tsp. crushed red pepper
4 cups sliced Swiss chard or spinach
Salt and pepper to taste
Polenta

Method

Combine all the ingredients, except Swiss chard, salt, pepper, and Polenta in 6-quart slow cooker. Now cover and cook on high heat for 3 to 4 hours. Now add Swiss chard during last 15 minutes. For seasoning add salt and pepper to taste. Serve over Polenta. Enjoy!

Veggie Stew with Bulgur

Ingredients

1 can (14 ½ ounces) diced tomatoes, undrained
1 cup spicy tomato juice
2 cups thickly sliced carrots
2 cups halved crimini mushrooms
1 cup chopped unpeeled Idaho potatoes
1 cup onion, chopped
1 thickly sliced medium red

1 thickly sliced medium green bell pepper
2–3 cloves garlic, minced
½ cup bulgur
1 tsp. tsp. dried thyme
1 tsp. oregano leaves
2 medium zucchini, cubed
1 medium yellow summer squash, cubed
Salt and pepper, to taste

Method

Combine all the ingredients, except zucchini, summer squash, salt, and pepper, in slow cooker. Now cover and cook on high heat for 4 to 5 hours, adding zucchini and summer squash during last 30 minutes. For seasoning add salt and pepper to taste. Enjoy!

Wheat Berry and Lentil Stew

Ingredients

3 cups reduced-sodium vegetable broth
1 cup wheat berries
½ cup dried lentils
1 ½ pounds russet potatoes, unpeeled, cubed
1 cup chopped onion
½ cup sliced carrots
½ cup celery
4 cloves garlic, minced
1 tsp. tsp. dried savory leaves
Salt and pepper, to taste

Method

Combine all ingredients, except salt and pepper, in 6-quart slow cooker; cover and cook on low 6 to 8 hours. For seasoning add salt and pepper to taste. Enjoy!

Lentil and Vegetable Stew

Ingredients

2 cups vegetable broth
8 small potatoes, cubed
3 cups sliced onions
3 cups chopped tomatoes
8 ounces chopped carrots
8 ounces green beans
½ cup dried lentils
2–4 small jalapeño or other hot chilies, mashed into a paste, or 1–2 tsp. cayenne pepper
1 tbsp. minced gingerroot
1 stick cinnamon
10 cloves garlic
6 whole cloves
6 crushed cardamom pods
1 tsp. tsp. ground turmeric
½ tsp. tsp. crushed dried mint leaves
Salt, to taste
2 cups frozen thawed peas
2 cups cooked warm couscous
Reduced-fat plain yogurt, as garnish

Method

Combine all the ingredients, except salt, peas, couscous, and yogurt in 6- quart slow cooker. Now cover and cook on low heat for 6 to 8 hours, adding peas during last 15 minutes. For seasoning add salt and pepper to taste. Serve over couscous and garnish it with dollops of yogurt. Enjoy!

Lentil Stew with Spiced Couscous

Ingredients

1 can (14 ½ ounces) diced tomatoes, undrained
3 cups reduced-sodium vegetable broth
2 cups dried lentils
1 cup chopped onion
1 cup chopped red or green bell pepper
1 cup chopped celery

1 cup chopped carrots
1 tsp. tsp. minced garlic
1 tsp. dried oregano leaves
½ tsp. ground turmeric
Salt and pepper, to taste
Spiced Couscous (recipe provided in this book)

Combine all the ingredients, except salt, pepper, and couscous, in 6-quart slow cooker. Now cover and cook on low heat for 6 to 8 hours. For seasoning add salt and pepper to taste. Serve over Spiced Couscous. Enjoy!

Spiced Couscous

Ingredients

1/3 cup sliced green onions
1 clove garlic, minced
1/8–1/4 tsp. crushed red pepper
½ tsp. tsp. ground turmeric
1 tsp. tsp. olive oil
1 2/3 cups reduced-sodium vegetable broth
1 cup couscous

Method

Sauté the green onions, garlic, red pepper, and turmeric in oil in medium saucepan for 3 minutes or until onions are tender. Stir in broth and heat to boiling. Now stir in couscous and remove from heat and let stand, covered for 5 minutes or until broth is absorbed. Enjoy!

Bean-Thickened Vegetable Stew

Pureed beans provide the perfect thickening for this stew.

Ingredients

1 ½ cups Basic Vegetable Stock (see p. 34) or vegetable broth
1 can (15 ounces) rinsed drained black
1 can (15 ounces) puréed navy beans
2 cups chopped tomatoes
1 ½ cups sliced mushrooms
1 yellow summer squash, sliced
½ cup sliced carrots
½ cup chopped onion
3 cloves garlic, minced
2 bay leaves
¾ tsp. tsp. dried thyme
¾ tsp. oregano leaves
1 cup frozen peas, thawed

Salt and pepper, to taste   4 cups cooked noodles, warm

Method

Combine all the ingredients, except peas, salt, pepper, and noodles, in slow cooker. Now cover and cook on high heat for 4 to 5 hours, adding peas during last 15 minutes. Discard bay leaves. For seasoning add salt and pepper to taste. Serve over noodles. Enjoy!

Chicken Stock

Ingredients

1 quart water
3 pounds chicken pieces
2 ribs celery, thickly sliced
3 thickly sliced small onions
3 thickly sliced medium carrots
1 small turnip, quartered
5 cloves garlic
2 bay leaves
½ tsp. tsp. whole peppercorns
1 tsp. tsp. dried sage leaves
Salt and pepper, to taste

Method

Combine all the ingredients, except salt and pepper, in slow cooker. Now cover and cook on low heat for 6 to 8 hours. For seasoning add salt and pepper to taste. Refrigerate stock overnight. Now skim fat from surface of stock and serve. Enjoy!

Rich Chicken Stock

Ingredients

4 quarts water
1 cup dry white wine or water
1 chicken (about 3 pounds), cut up, fat trimmed
1 veal knuckle, cracked (optional)
2 thickly sliced medium onions
2 leeks (white parts only)
4 thickly sliced medium carrots
4 thickly ribs celery

1 clove garlic, peeled
½ tsp. tsp. dried basil
½ tsp. thyme
½ tsp. tarragon leaves
10 black peppercorns
4 whole cloves
Salt and pepper, to taste

Method

Combine all the ingredients, except salt and pepper, in 6-quart slow cooker. Now cover and cook on low heat for 6 to 8 hours. Strain stock through double layer of cheesecloth and discard solids. For seasoning add salt and pepper to taste. Refrigerate until chilled. Now remove fat from surface of stock and serve. Enjoy!

Turkey Stock

Ingredients

1 cup dry white wine or water
1 turkey carcass, cut up
2 thickly sliced medium onions
2 leeks (white parts only)
4 thickly sliced medium carrots
4 ribs celery
1 tsp. tsp. dried thyme leaves
10 black peppercorns
6 sprigs parsley
Salt and pepper, to taste

Method

Combine all the ingredients, except salt and pepper, in 6-quart slow cooker. Now cover and cook on low heat for 6 to 8 hours. Strain stock through double layer of cheesecloth and discard solids. For seasoning add salt and pepper to taste. Refrigerate until chilled, now remove fat from surface of stock and serve. Enjoy!

Beef Stock

Ingredients

2 ½ quarts water
2 ribs from cooked beef rib roast, fat trimmed

4 thickly sliced large onions
4 thickly sliced medium carrots
4 thickly sliced small ribs celery
1 parsnip, halved
2 bay leaves
8 black peppercorns
5 sage leaves
Salt, to taste

Method

Combine all the ingredients, except salt, in 6-quart slow cooker. Now cover and cook on low heat for 6 to 8 hours. Strain stock through double layer of cheesecloth and discard solids. For seasoning add salt to taste. Refrigerate until chilled, now remove fat from surface of stock and serve. Enjoy!

Fragrant Beef Stock

Ingredients

3 quarts water
1 cup dry red wine (optional)
2 pounds short ribs of beef (fat trimmed)
2 pounds beef marrow bones
1 pound cubed beef chuck, fat trimmed
1 large onion, chopped
3 thickly sliced medium carrots
3 thickly sliced ribs celery

½ cup dried mushrooms
1 clove garlic, halved
10 black peppercorns
1 bay leaf
1 tsp. tsp. dried basil
1 tsp. thyme leaves
1 tbsp. soy sauce
Salt, to taste

Method

Combine all the ingredients, except salt, in 6-quart slow cooker. Now cover and cook on low heat for 6 to 8 hours. Strain stock through double layer of cheesecloth now discard solids. For seasoning add salt to taste. Refrigerate until chilled. Now remove fat from surface of stock and serve. Enjoy!

Veal Stock

Ingredients

2 quarts water
1 ½ pounds veal cubes for stew
½ cup chopped onion

½ cup chopped carrot
½ cup chopped celery
1 veal knuckle or veal bones (about 1¾ pounds)
2 bay leaves
6 black peppercorns
3 whole cloves
Salt and pepper, to taste

Method

Combine all the ingredients, except salt and pepper, in 6-quart slow cooker. Now cover and cook on low heat for 6 to 8 hours. Strain through double layer of cheesecloth and discard solids. For seasoning add salt and pepper to taste. Refrigerate until chilled, now remove fat from surface of the stock and serve. Enjoy!

Fish Stock

Ingredients

1 ½ quarts water
2–3 pounds fish bones (from non-oily fish)
1 chopped large onion
1 rib celery
2 bay leaves
7–8 black peppercorns
½ tsp. tsp. kosher or sea salt
½ tsp. white pepper

Method

Combine all the ingredients in slow cooker and cook on low heat for 4 to 6 hours. Strain through double layer of cheesecloth, and discard solids. Ready to serve. Enjoy!

Easy Fish Stock

Ingredients

3 ½ cups water
¾ cup dry white wine or water
1 ½ pounds fresh or frozen fish steaks, cubed (1-inch)
1 finely chopped medium onion
1 finely chopped carrot
3 ribs celery with leaves, halved

3 sprigs parsley
3 slices lemon
8 black peppercorns
Salt, to taste

Method

Combine all the ingredients, except salt, in slow cooker Now cover and cook on low heat for 4 to 6 hours. Strain stock through double layer of cheesecloth and discard solids. For seasoning add salt to taste. Enjoy!

Basic Vegetable Stock

Ingredients

2 quarts water
1 cup dry white wine or water
1 thickly sliced large onion
1 thickly sliced leek (white part only)
1 sliced carrot
1 rib celery
4 cups mixed chopped vegetables (broccoli, green beans, cabbage, potatoes, tomatoes, summer or winter squash, bell peppers, mushrooms, etc.)
6–8 parsley sprigs
1 bay leaf
4 whole allspice
1 tbsp. black peppercorns
2 tsp. dried bouquet garni
Salt, to taste

Method

Combine all the ingredients, except salt, in 6-quart slow cooker, now cover and cook on high heat for 3 to 4 hours or low heat for 6 to 8 hours. Strain stock, and discard solids. For seasoning add salt to taste. Now ready to serve. Enjoy!

Roasted Vegetable Stock

Ingredients

2 quarts water
1 cup dry white wine or water
1 coarsely chopped medium onion

1 leek (white part only)
1 carrot, chopped
1 zucchini, chopped

1 turnip, chopped
1 beet, chopped
1 tomato, chopped
½ small butternut or acorn squash, cubed
(2-inch)
1 bulb garlic, cut crosswise in half
3 cups coarsely chopped kale

6 sprigs parsley
1 bay leaf
1–2 tsp. dried bouquet garni
1 tsp. tsp. black peppercorns
4 whole allspice
Salt and pepper, to taste

Method

Arrange the vegetables, except kale, in single layer on greased, foil-lined jelly roll pan. Now bake it at 425 degrees F until tender and browned, 35 to 40 minutes. Transfer vegetables to 6-quart slow cooker and add remaining ingredients, except salt and pepper. Now cover and cook on low heat for 4 to 6 hours. Strain, and discard solids. For seasoning add salt and pepper to taste. Enjoy!

Garlic-Rosemary Cashews

Ingredients

6 cups cashews
3 tbsp.. margarine or butter, melted
1 tbsp. sugar
3 tbsp.. crushed dried rosemary leaves
¾ tsp. tsp. cayenne pepper
½ tsp. tsp. garlic powder

Method

Heat slow cooker on high heat for 15 minutes now add cashews. Drizzle margarine over cashews and toss it well, now add remaining ingredients and toss. Cover and cook on low heat for 2 hours, keep stirring every hour. Turn heat to high, now uncover and cook 30 minutes, keep stirring on intervals after 15 minutes. Turn heat to low to keep warm for serving or remove from slow cooker and cool. Enjoy!

Garlic-Pepper Almonds

Ingredients

6 cups whole unblanched almonds
4 tbsp.. margarine or butter, melted
3 cloves garlic, minced
2–3 tsp. coarse ground pepper

Method

Heat slow cooker on high heat for 15 minutes now add almonds. Drizzle margarine over almonds and toss well. Now sprinkle with garlic and pepper and toss. Cover and cook on low heat for 2 hours, keep stirring every 30 minutes. Turn heat to high, then uncover and cook 30 minutes, keep stirring after 15 minutes. Turn heat to low to keep warm for serving or remove from slow cooker and cool. Enjoy!

Sugar-Glazed Five-Spice Pecans

Ingredients

8 tbsp.. margarine or butter, melted
½ cup powdered sugar
1 tsp. tsp. ground cinnamon
¾ tsp. tsp. five-spice powder
6 cups pecan halves

Method

Heat the slow cooker on high heat for 15 minutes. Mix margarine, sugar, and spices and pour over pecans in large bowl and toss it well. Transfer mixture to slow cooker, now cover and cook on high heat for 30 minutes. Uncover and cook until pecans are crisply glazed, 45 to 60 minutes, keep stirring every 20 minutes. Pour pecans in single layer on jelly roll pans and cool. Enjoy!

Curry-Spiced Mixed Nuts

Ingredients

6 cups mixed nuts
4 tbsp.. margarine or butter, melted
2 tbsp.. sugar
1 ½ tsp. curry powder
1 tsp. tsp. garlic powder
1 tsp. ground cinnamon

Method

Heat the slow cooker on high heat for 15 minutes, then add nuts. Drizzle margarine over nuts and toss well. Now sprinkle with combined remaining ingredients and toss. Cover and cook on low heat for 2 hours, and keep stirring every 20 minutes. Turn heat to high, uncover and cook 30 minutes, keep stirring after 15 minutes. Turn heat to low to keep warm for serving or remove from slow cooker and cool. Enjoy!

Sweet Curried Soy Nuts

Ingredients

4 tbsp.. margarine or butter, melted
6 cups roasted soy nuts
1 ½ tbsp.. sugar
1 tbsp. curry powder
Salt, to taste

Method

Heat the slow cooker on high heat for 15 minutes. Drizzle margarine over soy nuts in large bowl and toss it well. Now sprinkle with combined remaining ingredients, except salt, and toss well. Transfer to slow cooker, now cover and cook on low heat for 2 hours, keep stirring every 15 minutes. Turn heat to high and remove the lid and cook 30 minutes, keep stirring after 15 minutes. For seasoning add salt to taste. Turn heat to low to keep warm for serving or remove from slow cooker and cool. Enjoy!

Soy Noshers

Ingredients

1 ½ cups roasted soy beans
½ cup wheat squares cereal
½ cup mini pretzel twists
1 cup dried cranberries or blueberries
Vegetable cooking spray
¾ tsp. tsp. crushed dried rosemary
¾ tsp. thyme leaves
Garlic salt, to taste

Method

Heat the slow cooker on high heat for 15 minutes and add soy beans, cereal, pretzels, and cranberries. Spray mixture generously with cooking spray and toss well, now sprinkle with herbs and toss. Cover and cook on low heat for 2 hours, keep stirring every 20 minutes. Turn heat to high, now uncover and cook 30 minutes, keep stirring after 15 minutes. For seasoning add garlic salt to taste. Turn heat to low to keep warm for serving or remove from slow cooker and cool. Enjoy!

Gorp, by Golly!

Ingredients

3 cups low-fat granola
2 cups pretzel goldfish
½ cup sesame sticks, broken into halves
3 cups coarsely chopped mixed dried fruit
Butter-flavored cooking spray
1 tsp. tsp. ground cinnamon
½ tsp. tsp. ground nutmeg

Method

Heat the slow cooker on high heat for 15 minutes, now add granola, goldfish, sesame sticks, and dried fruit. Spray mixture generously with cooking spray and toss well, then sprinkle with combined spices and toss. Cook, uncovered, on high heat for 1 ½ hours, stirring every 30 minutes. Turn slow cooker to low to keep warm for serving or remove from slow cooker and cool. Enjoy!

Hot Stuff!

Ingredients

4 cups baked pita chips
2 cups oyster crackers
½ cup dry-roasted smoked almonds
1 cup coarsely chopped mixed dried fruit
1 cup dried pineapple chunks
Butter-flavored cooking spray
1 tsp. tsp. dried oregano leaves
1 tsp. garlic powder
1 tsp. chili powder
1 tsp. cayenne pepper
1 tsp. black pepper

Method

Heat the slow cooker on high heat for 15 minutes, now add pita chips, crackers, almonds, and dried fruit. Spray mixture generously with cooking spray and toss. Now sprinkle with combined herbs and pepper and toss. Now uncover and cook on high 1 ½ hours, stirring every 30 minutes. Turn slow cooker to low to keep warm for serving or remove from slow cooker and cool. Enjoy!

Favorite Party Mix

Ingredients

5 cups assorted cereal (rice, oats, and wheat)
1 ½ cups small pretzels
1 ½ sesame sticks
1 ½ mixed nuts
¼ cup margarine or butter, melted
3 tbsp.. Worcestershire sauce
1 tsp. hot pepper sauce
1 tbsp. dried minced onion
½ tsp. tsp. garlic powder
Salt, to taste

Method

Heat the slow cooker on high heat for 15 minutes, now add cereal, pretzels, sesame sticks, and mixed nuts. Then drizzle with combined remaining ingredients, except salt, and toss. Now uncover and cook on high heat for 1 ½ hours, keep stirring every 30 minutes. For seasoning add salt to taste. Turn slow cooker to low to keep warm for serving or remove from slow cooker and cool. Enjoy!

Hot Curried Party Mix

Ingredients

3 cups rice cereal squares
1 cup sesame sticks
½ cup cashews
½ cup honey roasted peanuts
½ cup wasabi peas
2 tbsp.. margarine or butter, melted
1 ½ tsp. soy sauce
1 ½ tsp. curry powder
1 ½ tsp. sugar

Method

Heat the slow cooker on high heat for 15 minutes, and add cereal, sesame sticks, nuts, and wasabi peas. Drizzle mixture with combined margarine and soy sauce and toss well. Now sprinkle with combined curry powder and sugar and toss. Now uncover and cook on high heat for 1 ½ hours, stirring every 30 minutes. Turn slow cooker to low to keep warm for serving or remove from slow cooker and cool. Enjoy!

Fennel-Scented Fish Stew

Ingredients

1 quart Fish Stock (see p. 33) or clam juice
1 cup dry white wine (optional)
5 medium tomatoes, peeled, chopped
1 cup chopped carrots
1 cup onion
3 cloves garlic, minced

1 tbsp. minced orange zest
1 tsp. tsp. fennel seeds, lightly crushed
2 pounds from fish fillets (cod, red snapper, salmon, orange roughly halibut), cut into pieces (11-inch)
1 cup chopped parsley
Salt and pepper, to taste

Method

Combine all the ingredients, except fish, parsley, salt, and pepper, in a slow cooker. Now cover and cook on low heat for 6 to 8 hours, then add the fish during last 15 minutes. Stir in parsley. For seasoning add salt and pepper to taste. Enjoy!

Aioli

Ingredients

3 cup reduced-fat mayonnaise
1 tsp. tsp. tarragon vinegar
1 tsp. lemon juice
1 tsp. tsp. Dijon mustard
3 cloves garlic, minced
Salt and white pepper, to taste

Method

Mix all the ingredients, except salt and white pepper in slow cooker. Now cover and cook on high heat for 4 to 5 hours. For seasoning add salt and pepper to taste. Enjoy!

Fish Stew Marsala

Ingredients

21 cups reduced-sodium fat-free chicken broth
1 cup dry Marsala wine or chicken broth
1 cup tomato paste
1 cup chopped onion
1 cup red bell peppers
1 cup green bell peppers

1 cup chopped celery
1 tsp. tsp. minced garlic
1 tsp. tsp. dried thyme leaves
1 pound haddock steaks, cubed (2-inch)
2 cups cooked medium pasta shells, warm
2–3 tbsp.. lemon juice
Salt and pepper, to taste

Method

Combine the all ingredients, except fish, pasta, lemon juice, salt, and pepper, in slow cooker. Now cover and cook on high heat for 4 to 5 hours, then add fish and pasta during last 10 to 15 minutes. For seasoning add lemon juice, salt and pepper to taste. Enjoy!

Seafood Stew with Risotto, Milanese-Style

Ingredients

1 can (141 ounces) diced tomatoes, undrained
1 cup reduced-sodium fat-free chicken broth
1 medium onion, chopped
1 clove garlic, minced
1 tsp. tsp. crushed saffron threads (optional)

1 cup sliced zucchini
8 ounces bay scallops
8 ounces peeled deveined medium shrimp
Microwave Risotto (recipe follows), warm
1 cup (1 ounce) grated Parmesan cheese
Salt and pepper, to taste

Method

Combine the tomatoes with liquid, 1 cup broth, onion, garlic, and saffron in slow cooker. Now cover and cook on high heat for 3 to 4 hours, then add zucchini during last 30 minutes and seafood during last 10 minutes. Stir in Microwave Risotto and Parmesan cheese, add the remaining 1 cup broth, if desired. For seasoning add salt and pepper to taste. Enjoy!

Microwave Risotto

Ingredients

3 cup uncooked arbor rice
2 tsp. olive oil
22 cups reduced-sodium fat-free chicken broth
1 tsp. tsp. dried thyme leaves
Salt and white pepper

Method

Combine all the ingredients in a slow cooker and cook on low heat for an hour or so or until the rice is cooked. Serve hot. Enjoy!

Scallop Stew, Italian-Style

Ingredients

1 can (141 ounces) Italian-style plum tomatoes, undrained, chopped
1 cup reduced-sodium fat-free chicken broth
1 cup chopped medium onion
1 cup chopped medium green bell pepper
1 minced clove garlic
1 bay leaf

1 tsp. tsp. dried basil leaves
2 cups small broccoli florets
12–16 ounces bay or sea scallops
2 tsp. cornstarch
1 cup cold water
2–4 tbsp.. dry sherry (optional)
Salt and pepper, to taste
1 cup cooked white or brown rice, warm

Method

Combine tomatoes with liquid, broth, onion, bell pepper, garlic, and herbs in a slow cooker Now cover and cook on high heat for 4 to 5 hours, the add broccoli during last 30 minutes and scallops during last 5 to 10 minutes. Stir in combined cornstarch and water, keep stirring for 2 to 3 minutes. Discard bay leaf and for seasoning add sherry, salt and pepper to taste. Serve over rice. Enjoy!

Italian-Style Fish Stew

Ingredients

1 cup reduced-sodium fat-free chicken broth or clam juice
1 cup dry white wine or chicken broth

11 pounds tomatoes, peeled, chopped
1 cup halved small mushrooms
3 large cloves garlic, minced

2 tsp. dried Italian seasoning
1 tsp. tsp. crushed red pepper
1 pound grouper or other from-fleshed fish steaks, thinly sliced

1 cup chopped parsley
Salt and pepper, to taste

Method

Combine all the ingredients, except fish, parsley, salt, and pepper, in a slow cooker. Now cover and cook on high heat for 4 to 5 hours, then add fish and parsley during last 10 minutes. For seasoning add salt and pepper to taste. Enjoy!

Mediterranean Fisherman's Stew

Ingredients

1 can (28 ounces) Italian plum tomatoes, undrained, chopped
1 cup clam juice
1 large onion, chopped
1 cup sliced carrots
4 tsp. minced garlic

1 tsp. tsp. dried basil leaves
1 tsp. tsp. lemon pepper
2 medium zucchini, cubed
1 pound cod, cubed (1-inch)
1 cup chopped parsley
Salt and pepper, to taste

Method

Combine all the ingredients, except zucchini, cod, parsley, salt, and pepper, in a slow cooker. Now cover and cook on high heat for 4 to 5 hours, then add zucchini during last 45 minutes and cod during last 10 minutes. Stir in parsley, and for seasoning add salt and pepper to taste. Enjoy!

Paella

Ingredients

8 ounces chicken tenders, halved
3 ounces Canadian bacon, cut into thin strips
21 cups reduced-sodium fat-free chicken broth
1 can (141 ounces) Italian-style diced tomatoes, undrained
1 can (143 ounces) artichoke hearts, drained, halved
1 cup chopped onion

1 cup red and green bell pepper
2 cloves garlic, minced
3 tsp. tsp. dried thyme
3 tsp. basil leaves
1 tsp. tsp. crushed saffron threads (optional)
11 cups uncooked converted long-grain rice
8 ounces medium shrimp, peeled, deviant
Salt and cayenne pepper, to taste

Method

Combine all the ingredients, except rice, shrimp, salt, and cayenne pepper, in slow cooker. Now cover and cook on low heat for 6 to 8 hours, then add rice during last 2 hours, and shrimp during last 10 minutes. For seasoning add salt and pepper to taste. Enjoy!

Thai-Style Shrimp Stew

Ingredients

2 cups reduced-sodium fat-free chicken broth, chopped
1 cup sliced red bell pepper
1 cup sliced scallions
1 cup fresh or canned rinsed drained bean sprouts

4 ounces bean threads or cellophane noodles, cut (2-inch)
1 cup rice wine vinegar
1 tsp. tsp. Chinese chili sauce with garlic
1 pound medium shrimp, peeled, deveined
Soy sauce, to taste
Salt and pepper, to taste

Method

Combine the broth and vegetables in slow cooker. Now cover and cook on high heat for 4 to 5 hours. While stew is cooking, soak cellophane noodles in hot water until softened. Drain it and add noodles, vinegar, chili sauce, and shrimp to slow cooker during last 10 minutes. For seasoning add soy sauce, salt and pepper to taste. Enjoy!

Shrimp and Vegetable Stew

Ingredients

1 can (141 ounces) stewed tomatoes
4 ounces smoked turkey sausage, thickly sliced
1 cup halved baby carrots
1 cup small Brussels sprouts
1 cup whole-kernel corn
1 medium onion, cut into thin wedges
1 tsp. tsp. chili powder
12–16 ounces medium shrimp, peeled, deveined
Salt and pepper, to taste
3 cups cooked rice, warm

Method

Combine all the ingredients, except shrimp, salt, pepper, and rice, in a slow cooker. Now cover and cook on high heat for 4 to 5 hours, then add shrimp during the last 10 to 15 minutes. For seasoning add salt and pepper to taste. Serve over rice. Enjoy!

Herbed Shrimp Stew

Ingredients

1 can (28 ounces) diced tomatoes with garlic, undrained
1 cup clam juice or vegetable broth
1 finely chopped medium onion
1 rib celery
2 cloves garlic, minced

1 tsp. tsp. dried thyme
1 tsp. basil leaves
1 cup chopped parsley
1 pound medium shrimp, peeled, deveined
3 cups cooked rice, warm
Salt and pepper, to taste

Method

Combine all the ingredients, except parsley, shrimp, rice, salt, and pepper, in slow a cooker. Now cover and cook on high heat for 3 to 4 hours, then add parsley, shrimp, and rice during last 10 minutes. For seasoning add salt and pepper to taste. Enjoy!

Spicy Shrimp and Rice Stew

Ingredients

2 cups reduced-sodium fat-free chicken broth
1 can (14 ounces) diced tomatoes, undrained
1 chopped large onion
1 carrot
1 rib celery
1 medium green bell pepper
2 large cloves garlic, minced
1 bay leaf
11 tsp. dried thyme leaves
3 tsp. tsp. paprika
3 cups cooked white rice, warm
1 pound medium shrimp, peeled, deveined
Salt, cayenne, and black pepper, to taste

Method

Combine all the ingredients, except rice, shrimp, salt, and pepper, in a slow cooker. Now cover and cook on high heat for 4 to 5 hours, then add rice and shrimp during last 10 to 15 minutes. Discard bay leaf; season to taste with salt, cayenne, and black pepper. Enjoy!

Shrimp, Artichoke, and Pepper Stew

Ingredients

1 can (14 ounces) reduced-sodium chunky tomato sauce
1 can (14 ounces) quartered artichoke hearts, drained
3 cups chicken or vegetable broth
3 cups thinly sliced onion
3 cups red and green bell pepper

1 tsp. tsp. minced garlic
12 ounces medium shrimp, peeled, deveined
1–2 tbsp.. dry sherry (optional)
Salt and pepper, to taste
8 ounces penne, cooked, warm

Method

Combine all the ingredients, except shrimp, sherry, salt, pepper, and penne, in a slow cooker. Now cover and cook on low heat for 5 to 6 hours, then add shrimp during last 10 minutes. For seasoning add sherry, salt and pepper to taste. Serve over penne. Enjoy!

Scallop, Shrimp, and Pepper Stew with Pasta

Ingredients

11 cups clam juice or reduced-sodium fat-free chicken broth
2 cups diced mixed red, yellow, and green bell peppers (1-inch)
1 cup coarsely chopped onion
1 cup tomato
2 large cloves garlic, minced
1 tsp. tsp. grated lemon zest

1 tsp. tsp. dried thyme leaves
Pinch crushed red pepper
8 ounces peeled deveined medium shrimp
8 ounces bay scallops
1 cup chopped fresh parsley
2–3 tsp. lemon juice
Salt and pepper, to taste
8 ounces vermicelli, cooked, warm

Method

Combine all ingredients, except seafood, parsley, lemon juice, salt, pepper, and pasta, in slow cooker; cover and cook on high 4 to 5 hours. Add seafood and parsley during the last 10 minutes. Season to taste with lemon juice, salt, and pepper. Serve over pasta. Enjoy!

Creole Stew with Shrimp and Ham

Ingredients

4 ounces lean ham, cut into thin strips
1–2 tbsp.. canola oil
1 can (28 ounces) stewed tomatoes
1 cup clam juice or water
2–3 tbsp.. tomato paste
1 cup finely chopped onion
1 cup celery

1cup red or green bell pepper
3 cloves garlic, minced
11 pounds shrimp, peeled, deveined
2–4 tbsp.. dry sherry (optional)
1 tsp. hot pepper sauce
Salt and pepper, to taste
4 cups cooked rice, warm

Method

Cook ham in oil in small skillet over medium-high heat until browned and crisp. Remove from heat and keep aside. Combine the tomatoes, clam juice, vegetables, and garlic a in slow cooker; cover and cook on high 3 to 4 hours. Add reserved ham, shrimp, sherry and hot pepper sauce during the last 10 minutes. Season to taste with salt and pepper; serve over rice. Enjoy!

Cajun Shrimp, Corn, and Bean Stew

Ingredients

1 can (15 ounces) red beans, rinsed, drained
1 can (16 ounces) cream-style corn
1 cup clam juice or chicken broth
1 finely chopped medium onion
1 minced jalapeño chili
2 cloves garlic, minced
1 tsp. dried thyme leaves

1 tsp. tsp. dried oregano leaves
1 cup small broccoli forests
1 cup whole milk
2 tbsp.. cornstarch
12–16 ounces shrimp, peeled, deveined
Salt, to taste
Hot pepper sauce, to taste

Method

Combine the beans, corn, clam juice, onion, jalapeño chili, garlic, and herbs in a slow cooker; cover and cook on high 3 to 4 hours. Add broccoli during the last 20 minutes. Stir in combined milk and cornstarch, keep stirring 2 to 3 minutes. Add shrimp; cook 5 to 10 minutes. For seasoning add salt and hot pepper sauce. Enjoy!

Shrimp and Sausage Gumbo

Ingredients

2 cans (14 ounces each) stewed tomatoes
4 ounces reduced-fat smoked sausage thickly sliced
1 large red bell pepper, finely chopped
1 clove garlic, minced
1 tsp. tsp. crushed red pepper

8 ounces fresh or frozen thawed sliced okra
8–12 ounces shrimp, peeled, deveined
Salt, to taste
3 cups cooked rice, warm

Method

Combine all the ingredients, except okra, shrimp, salt, and rice, in a slow cooker; cover and cook on low 6 to 7 hours. Add okra during the last 30 minutes and shrimp during the last 10 minutes. For seasoning add salt and pepper to taste; serve over rice. Enjoy!

Rouladen

Thin sandwich steaks make easy work of Rouladen.

Ingredients

4 small or 2 large thin beef sandwich steaks (about 1 pound)
Salt and pepper, to taste
4 slices smoked ham (about 1 ounce each)
1 cup finely chopped mushrooms

1 cup each: finely chopped dill pickle, onion
1–2 tbsp.. Dijon mustard
1 tsp. tsp. dried dill weed
1 cup beef broth

Methods

Sprinkle the sandwich steaks lightly with salt and pepper; top each steak with the ham slice. Mix the remaining ingredients, except broth, and spread over the ham slices. Roll up steaks, securing with toothpicks; place, seam sides down, in a slow cooker. Add broth; cover and cook on low 5 to 6 hours. Serve hot. Enjoy!

Just Plain Meat Loaf

Ingredients

11 pounds lean ground beef
1 cup quick-cooking oats
1 cup 2% reduced-fat milk

1 egg
1 cup ketchup or chili sauce
1 cup chopped onion

1 cup green bell pepper
1 tsp. tsp. minced garlic
1 tsp. dried Italian seasoning

1 tsp. tsp. salt
1 tsp. tsp. pepper

Method

Make foil handles and put into a slow cooker. Mix all the ingredients until blended; pat mixture into a loaf shape and place in a slow cooker. make sure the sides of loaf do not touch crock. Insert meat thermometer so tip is in center of loaf; cover and cook on low until meat thermometer registers 170 degrees F, 6 to 7 hours. Remove, using foil handles, and let stand, loosely covered with foil, 10 minutes. Enjoy!

Braised Short Ribs

You'll find these short ribs especially tasty and juicy—nibbling on the bones is allowed!

Ingredients1

 cup dry red wine or beef broth
4 large carrots, thickly sliced
1 large onion, cut into wedges

2 bay leaves
1 tsp. tsp. dried marjoram
2 pounds beef short ribs

Method

Combine all the ingredients in a slow cooker. Place short ribs on the top; cover and cook on low 7 to 8 hours. Serve hot. Enjoy!

Lemon Meat Loaf

Ingredients

11 pounds lean ground beef
1 cup fresh bread crumbs
1 egg
1 cup chopped onion
1 cup green bell pepper
1 clove garlic, minced
1 tbsp. lemon juice

1 tbsp. grated lemon zest
1 tsp. tsp. Dijon mustard
1 tsp. tsp. dried savory leaves
1 tsp. pepper
3 tsp. tsp. salt
Egg Lemon Sauce (recipe follows)

Method

Make foil handles and put into slow cooker. Mix all the ingredients until blended; pat mixture into a loaf shape and place in slow cooker. Make sure the sides of loaf do not touch crock. Insert meat thermometer so tip is in center of loaf; cover and cook on low until meat thermometer registers 170 degrees, 6 to 7 hours. Remove, using foil handles, and let stand, loosely covered with foil, 10 minutes. Serve with Egg Lemon Sauce. Enjoy!

Egg Lemon Sauce

Ingredients

1 tbsp. margarine or butter
2 tbsp.. flour
1 cup reduced-sodium fat-free chicken broth
1 cup 2% reduced-fat milk

1 egg, lightly beaten
3–4 tbsp.. lemon juice
1 tsp. tsp. grated lemon zest
Salt and white pepper, to taste

Method

Melt the margarine in a medium saucepan; whisk in four and cook 1 minute. Whisk in broth and milk; heat to boiling, keep whisking until thickened, about 1 minute. Whisk about the broth mixture into the egg; whisk mixture back into saucepan. Whisk over medium heat 1 minute. Add lemon juice and zest; season to taste with salt and white pepper. Enjoy!

Stuffed Cabbage Leaves

You'll enjoy this hearty dish that's stuffed with ground beef and rice and sauced with tomatoes.

Ingredients

8 large cabbage leaves
1 pound lean ground beef
1 cup finely chopped onion
1 cup green bell pepper
1 cup cooked rice
1 cup water

1 tsp. tsp. salt
1 tsp. tsp. pepper
1 can (14 ounces) tomato sauce
1 can (16 ounces) petite-diced tomatoes, undrained

Method

Place the cabbage leaves in boiling water until softened, 1 to 2 minutes, and drain well. Trim thick veins from leaves so they lay fat. Mix ground beef and remaining ingredients, except tomato sauce and diced tomatoes. Divide meat mixture into 8 equal parts, shaping each into a loaf shape; wrap each in a cabbage leaf, folding ends and sides over. Pour half the combined tomato sauce and diced tomatoes with liquid into slow cooker. Add the cabbage rolls, seam sides down. Pour remaining tomato mixture over; cover and cook on low 6 to 8 hours. Enjoy!

Meatballs Florentine

Ingredients

1 cup spinach leaves
1 cup ricotta cheese
1 egg
1 cup chopped green onions
2 cloves garlic
2 tsp. tsp. dried oregano leaves
1 tsp. tsp. dried dill leaves

1 tsp. ground nutmeg
1 tsp. salt, pepper
1 pound lean ground beef
1 cup fresh bread crumbs
4 cups spaghetti sauce with herbs
8 ounces fettuccine, cooked, warm

Method

Process the spinach, ricotta cheese, egg, green onions, garlic, seasonings, salt, and pepper in food processor until smooth. Mix it with ground beef and bread crumbs. Shape mixture into 8 to 12 meatballs. Combine meatballs and spaghetti sauce in a slow cooker, covering meatballs with sauce. Cover and cook on low 5 to 6 hours. Serve on fettuccine. Enjoy!

Ziti with Eggplant Meatballs

Eggplant Meatballs (recipe follows)

Ingredients

12 ounces ziti or other shaped pasta, cooked, warm
2–3 tbsp.. olive oil

2 tbsp.. drained capers
1 cup chopped Italian parsley

Method

Make Eggplant Meatballs. Toss ziti with oil, capers, and parsley; serve with meatballs. Enjoy!

Eggplant Meatballs

Ingredients

1 small eggplant (about 12 ounces), peeled, cubed
11 pounds lean ground beef
1 cup grated Romano cheese (2 ounces)
1 cup unseasoned dry bread crumbs

2 eggs
11 tsp. dried Italian seasoning
1 tsp. tsp. salt
1 tsp. tsp. pepper
1 jar (26 ounces) spaghetti sauce

Method

Cook the eggplant in 2 inches simmering water in medium saucepan until tender, about 10 minutes; drain, cool, and mash. Combine the eggplant with remaining ingredients, except spaghetti sauce; shape into 18 meatballs. Combine meatballs and spaghetti sauce in a slow cooker, covering meatballs with sauce. Cover and cook on high 3 to 4 hours. Enjoy!

Veal Meatballs with Sour-Cream Mushroom Sauce

Ingredients

8 ounces sliced mushrooms
Veal Meatballs (recipe follows)
1 cup chicken broth
1 cup reduced-fat sour cream

3 tbsp.. cornstarch
Salt and pepper, to taste
8 ounces fettuccine, cooked, warm

Method

Place 3 of the mushrooms in bottom of a slow cooker; top with meatballs and remaining mushrooms. Pour broth over; cover and cook on low 5 to 6 hours. Remove meatballs and keep warm. Stir combined sour cream and cornstarch into broth, keep stirring 2 to 3 minutes. Season to taste with salt and pepper. Serve meatballs and sauce over fettuccine. Enjoy!

Veal Meatballs

Ingredients

11 pounds ground veal
1 cup finely chopped green onions
1 clove garlic
2 eggs

1 cup chicken broth or milk
1 cup unseasoned dry bread crumbs
1 tsp. tsp. salt
1 tsp. tsp. pepper

Method

Mix all ingredients; shape into 8 meatballs. Enjoy!

Fruit-Stuffed Pork Loin

Ingredients

3 cup pitted prunes

1 boneless pork loin roast (about 2 pounds)

1 cup chopped peeled apple
1 tsp. tsp. dried marjoram
1 tsp. sage leaves
Salt and pepper, to taste

1 cup dry white wine or apple juice
2 tbsp.. each: cornstarch, honey
3 cup whole milk or light cream

Method

Soak the prunes in hot water to cover until softened, 10 to 15 minutes. Drain well; now chop coarsely. Push the handle of a long wooden spoon through the center of the roast to make an opening for the stuffing. Combine prunes, apple, and herbs; push mixture through meat, using the handle of a wooden spoon. Sprinkle outside of the roast lightly with salt and pepper; place meat thermometer in roast, making sure tip does not rest in stuffing. Place pork and wine in a slow cooker; cover and cook on low until temperature registers 160 degrees F, about 3 hours. Remove meat to platter and keep warm; turn heat to high and cook 10 minutes. Stir in the combined cornstarch, honey, and milk, stirring 2 to 3 minutes. Enjoy!

Pork Loin Braised in Milk

Ingredients

1 boneless pork loin roast (about 3 pounds)
Salt and pepper, to taste
1 cup whole milk

1 cup dry white wine or milk
2 rosemary, large
2 sage sprigs
2 cloves garlic, minced

Method

Sprinkle the pork lightly with salt and pepper; insert meat thermometer in center of roast so tip is in center of meat. Place meat and remaining ingredients in a slow cooker; cover and cook on low until meat thermometer registers 160 degrees F. Remove to serving platter. Strain broth, discarding milk curds and herbs; make gravy with broth or reserve for another use. Enjoy!

Pork Roast with Mango Chutney

Ingredients

1 cup finely chopped onion
1 cup chicken broth
1 boneless pork loin roast (about 3 pounds)
Mango Chutney (recipe follows)

Paprika
Salt and pepper

Method

Place the onion and broth in a slow cooker. Sprinkle the pork lightly with paprika, salt, and pepper; insert meat thermometer in center of roast so tip is in center of the meat. Place pork in a slow cooker; cover and cook on low until meat thermometer registers 160 degrees F. Now remove the pork to serve on platter and let stand, loosely covered with foil, 10 minutes. Make gravy with broth mixture or reserve for soup or another use. Serve pork with Mango Chutney. Enjoy!

Mango Chutney

Ingredients

3 cups chopped mango (about 3 mangoes)   1 large clove garlic, minced
1 cup packed light brown sugar   4 cardamom pods, crushed
1 cup cider vinegar   1 small stick cinnamon
1 cup white raisins   2 cloves
2 tsp. minced jalapeno chili   Salt, to taste
11 tbsp. minced ginger-root

Method

Combine all the ingredients in a slow cooker; cover and cook on high 3 hours. Uncover and cook until thickened to desired consistency, about 2 hours. Cool; refrigerate. Season to taste with salt. Enjoy!

Pork Loin with Mustard Sauce

Ingredients

1 cup chopped onion   Paprika
1 cup chicken broth   Salt and pepper
1 boneless pork loin roast (about 3   Mustard Sauce (recipe follows)
pounds)

Method

Place the onion and broth in a slow cooker. Sprinkle pork lightly with paprika, salt, and pepper; insert meat thermometer in center of roast so tip is in center of the meat. Place pork in a slow cooker; cover and cook on low until meat thermometer registers 160 degrees F. Now remove pork to serving platter and let stand, loosely covered with foil, 10 minutes. Strain broth and onions; spoon onions around pork. Reserve the broth for soup or another use. Serve pork with Mustard Sauce. Enjoy!

Mustard Sauce

Ingredients

1 cup sugar
1 cup dry mustard
1 tbsp. flour

1 cup cider vinegar
2 eggs
1 tbsp. margarine or butter

Method

Mix sugar, dry mustard, and flour in a small saucepan; whisk in vinegar and eggs. Cook over low heat until thickened, about 10 minutes; stir in margarine. Enjoy!

Pork Shoulder Roast with Noodles

Ingredients

1 cup chopped onion
1 cup chicken broth
1 boneless pork shoulder roast (about 3 pounds)

Salt and pepper
3 tbsp.. cornstarch
1 cup water
4–6 cups cooked noodles or rice, warm

Method

Place the onion and broth in a slow cooker. Sprinkle pork lightly with salt and pepper and place in the slow cooker; cover and cook on low 7 to 8 hours. Remove pork and shred. Turn slow cooker to high; cook 10 minutes. Stir in combined cornstarch and water, stirring 2 to 3 minutes. Return the pork to slow cooker and toss; serve over noodles or rice. Enjoy!

Herbed Pork Chops

Ingredients

4 boneless loin pork chops (4 ounces each)
1 tsp. tsp. dried thyme leaves
Salt and pepper, to taste
1 small onion, halved, sliced
4 green onions, thinly sliced
1 small rib celery, sliced
1 can (10 ounces) 98% fat-free cream of celery soup

1 cup 2% reduced fat milk

Method

Sprinkle the pork chops with thyme, salt, and pepper; place in slow cooker, now add onions and celery. Pour the combined soup and milk over; cover and cook on low 4 to 5 hours. Enjoy!

Pork Chops with Apricot-Hoisin Sauce

Ingredients

6 boneless loin pork chops (about 4 ounces each)
Salt and pepper, to taste
1 cup chicken broth

1 cup apricot preserves
3 tbsp.. hoisin sauce
2–3 tsp. cornstarch
2 tbsp.. finely chopped cilantro or parsley

Method

Sprinkle the pork chops very lightly with salt and pepper and place in slow cooker; add chicken broth. Cover and cook on low until pork chops are tender, about 3 hours, Now remove the pork chops and keep warm. Turn heat to high and cook 10 minutes; stir combined remaining ingredients into broth, stirring 2 to 3 minutes. Serve sauce over pork chops. Enjoy!

Pork Stewed with Prunes

Ingredients

2 pounds boneless pork loin, cubed (11-inch)
8 ounces pitted prunes
11 cups chicken broth
1 cup dry white wine or chicken broth
Grated zest of 1 lemon

2 tbsp.. cornstarch
1 cup cold water
1–2 tsp. lemon juice
Salt and pepper, to taste
4 cups cooked rice or couscous, warm

Method

Combine all the ingredients, except cornstarch, water, lemon juice, salt, pepper, and rice, in slow cooker; cover and cook on low 6 to 8 hours. Turn heat to high and cook 10 minutes; stir in the combined cornstarch and water, keep stirring 2 to 3 minutes. Season to taste with lemon juice, salt, and pepper; serve over rice. Enjoy!

Pork Chops with Sage

Ingredients

4 boneless loin pork chops (about 4 ounces each)
1 cup chopped onion
1 cup chicken broth
1 cup dry white wine or chicken broth

1 tbsp. cornstarch
2 tbsp.. each: honey, water
1–2 tbsp. Dijon mustard
1-2 tbsp. lemon juice
Salt and pepper, to taste

Method

Combine the pork chops, onion, broth, and wine in a slow cooker; cover and cook on low until pork chops are tender, 3 to 4 hours. Remove the pork chops and keep warm; turn heat to high. Stir the combined cornstarch, honey and water into broth; cook, uncovered, until juices are a thin sauce consistency, about 5 minutes. Season to taste with mustard, lemon juice, salt, and pepper. Enjoy!

Country-Style Ribs with Plum Sauce

Ingredients

3 pounds country-style pork ribs, cut into servings
1 jar (7 ounces) plum sauce
1 cup honey

1 tsp. soy sauce
2 tbsp.. cornstarch
1 cup orange juice
Salt and pepper, to taste

Method

Arrange the ribs in a slow cooker; pour the combined plum sauce, honey, and soy sauce over ribs. Cover and cook on low 6 to 8 hours. Remove the ribs to platter; keep warm. Turn heat to high and cook 10 minutes; stir in combined cornstarch and orange juice, keep stirring 2 to 3 minutes. Season it with salt and pepper; serve sauce over ribs. Enjoy!

Orange-Honey Ham

Ingredients

3 pounds boneless smoked ham
1 cup orange juice
1 cup honey
1 tsp. tsp. ground cloves

11 tbsp.. cornstarch
1 cup cold water
2 tbsp.. dry sherry (optional)

Method

Place the meat thermometer in ham so tip is near the center; place in a slow cooker. Add the remaining ingredients, except cornstarch, water, and sherry. Cover and cook on low until temperature registers 155 degrees F, about 3 hours. Remove the ham to a platter and keep warm. Measure 11 cups broth into saucepan and heat to boiling; whisk in combined cornstarch, water, and sherry, whisking until thickened, about 1 minute. Serve sauce over ham. Enjoy!

Busy Day Crockpot Chicken and Rice

Ingredients

1 lb. boneless skinless chicken breasts
2 cans 98% fat-free cream of chicken soup

1 can 98% fat-free cream of mushroom soup
1 box chicken flavor rice-a-roni

Method

Put the chicken and soups into the crock pot; cook on low for 8-10 hours. When you get home, cook the rice according to package directions. Serve the chicken and gravy over rice. Enjoy!

Cabbage Burger Bake

Ingredients

1 (1 lb.) package. (about 6 cups) shredded cabbage and carrots
¾ lb. lean ground beef
½ tsp. salt
¼ tsp. ground black pepper
1 medium onion, finely chopped

1 cup long-grain rice
1 (26 oz.) can chunky low-fat spaghetti sauce
½ cup water
¼ tsp. dried basil leaves, crushed
¼ tsp. seasoned salt

Method

Place 1/2 of the cabbage and carrots in a 3 1/2 quart slow cooker. Crumble ground beef over top. Sprinkle with salt and pepper. Evenly distribute onion, then rice over all. Top with the remaining cabbage, salt, and pepper. Combine spaghetti sauce, water, basil, and seasoned salt; pour over cabbage. Cover and cook on LOW 5 to 6 hours or until rice is tender. Enjoy!

Cafe Chicken

Ingredients

2 ½ pounds chicken breast halves without skin, cut into eighths
1 Onion,, chopped
2 garlic,, chopped
Salt & white pepper to taste

1 Green pepper,, diced
1 Medium Tomato, Ripe and Peeled,, Seeded and chopped
1 Cup Dry white wine,, 1 Pinch cayenne pepper

Method

Combine all the ingredients in slow-cooker. Cover pot and set at Low. Cook for 6 to 8 hours, or until chicken is tender. Enjoy!

Campbell 's One Dish Chicken & Rice

Ingredients

1 can cream of mushroom soup Campbell's 98% FF
1 cup water
¾ cup white rice, regular, uncooked
¼ tsp. tsp. paprika

¼ tsp. tsp. pepper
1 tsp. tsp. garlic salt, my own addition
4 chicken breast halves, skinned and boned

Method

In a 2 quart shallow baking dish, mix the soup, water, rice, paprika and pepper. Place the chicken on rice mixture. Sprinkle with additional paprika and pepper. Cover and bake at 375 degrees F for 45 minutes or until chicken and rice are done. For Creamier rice, increase water to 1 1/3 cups. Cheaters Chicken Cacciatore 6 skinless, boneless chicken breast halves 1 (28 ounce) jar spaghetti sauce 2 green bell pepper, seeded and cubed 8 ounces fresh mushrooms, sliced 1 onion, finely diced 2 tbsp. minced garlic Put the chicken in the slow cooker. Top with the spaghetti sauce, green bell peppers, mushrooms, onion and garlic. Cook on low for 7 to 9 hours. Serve. Enjoy!

Cheddar Fondue

Ingredients

¼ cup butter or margarine
¼ cup all-purpose flour
½ tsp. tsp. salt, optional

¼ tsp. tsp. pepper
¼ tsp. tsp. mustard powder
¼ tsp. tsp. Worcestershire sauce

1 ½ cups skim milk
2 cups shredded cheddar cheese
2 bread cubes

2 ham cubes
2 bite-size sausage

Method

Combine all the ingredients in a crock pot and heat on low for 1 hour. When done keep warm and transfer to a fondue pot and serve immediately. Enjoy!

Cheesy Artichoke Chicken and Pasta

Ingredients

1 lb. boneless skinless chicken breasts,, cubed (1 to 1 1/2)
4 oz. roasted red peppers,, chopped (4 to 6)
15 ounces artichoke hearts,, quartered
8 oz. fat-free American cheese

2 tsp. Worcestershire sauce
1 can 98% fat-free cream of mushroom soup
2 cups fat-free shredded cheddar cheese
4 cups hot cooked pasta
to taste salt and pepper

Method

In a 3 ½ quart or a larger crock pot combine the chicken, peppers, artichokes, American cheese, Worcestershire sauce, and soup in the crock pot. Cover and cook on low for 6 to 8 hours. About 15 minutes before serving, add shredded Cheddar cheese and hot cooked pasta. Taste and add salt and pepper as needed. Enjoy!

Cheesy Crockpot Chicken

Ingredients

2 lbs. boneless skinless chicken breasts
2 Cans 98% fat-free cream of chicken soup

1 can cheddar cheese soup
¼ tsp. tsp. garlic powder

Method

Cut the chicken into bite size pieces. Put the chicken in the bottom of the crock pot. Add rest of the ingredients on top. Cook 8 hours on low. Serve over rice or noodles. Enjoy!

Chicken & Rice

Ingredients

½ lb. mushrooms, fresh
½ cup onion
1 lb. chicken pieces
1 tsp. chicken bouillon

1 tsp. poultry seasoning
¼ tsp. salt
2 cups water
¾ cup rice, uncooked

Method

Slice the mushrooms. Remove skin the from chicken. Spray 12" skillet with nonstick spray coating. Brown mushrooms, onion, and the chicken pieces on all sides over medium heat about 15 minutes. Stir in the seasonings and transfer to crock pot. Refrigerated for overnight. Start crock pot on LOW. When ingredients are heated, add rice. Cook until done. Enjoy!

Chicken A La King

Ingredients

¼ cup onion, finely chopped,
¼ cup celery,, finely chopped
¼ cup green pepper,, finely chopped
¼ cup pimento, chopped
4 ounces mushroom stems and pieces, drained

3 cups chicken or turkey,, cooked and cubed
½ tsp. tsp. seasoned salt
1/8 tsp. tsp. pepper
1 (10 ounce) can cream of mushroom soup
1 (13 ounce can) evaporated skim milk

Method

Put all the ingredients into an electric slow cooker and mix. Cover and cook on low for 2 to 3 hours, or until thoroughly heated; stir once. Serve in patty shells or over hot fluffy rice. To reduce fat in this dish, use Campbell's Healthy Choice Cream of Mushroom Soup, chicken breast meat cooked without fat, nonfat evaporated milk and serve over white or brown rice cooked without added fat. Enjoy!

Chicken and Stuffing

Ingredients

6 whole boneless skinless chicken breasts
1 box stove top stuffing mix

1 can 98% fat-free cream of mushroom soup, or any cream soup
½ cup water or chicken bouillon

Method

Spray a 3 1/2 quart crock pot with cooking spray. Add the chicken breasts. Combine stuffing, soup, and liquid. Spread over chicken. Cook on low 6 – 8 hours. Serve hot.

Chicken Brunswick Stew

Ingredients

2 tbsp. flour
2 tsp. instant bouillon granules, chicken flavor
1 ½ tsp. poultry seasoning
¼ tsp. pepper
6 bone in chicken thighs (about 2 lbs.)
2 medium potatoes cut in 1" pieces

½ cup chopped onion
1 (15-oz.) can tomato sauce
1 tbsp. Worcestershire
1 (9-oz.) package green giant frozen baby lima beans, thawed
1 (9-oz.) package green giant frozen niblets corn, thawed

Method

In large re-sealable food storage plastic bag, combine the flour, bouillon, poultry seasoning and pepper and mix well. Add the chicken thighs, potatoes and onion; seal the bag and shake well to coat. Place in a slow cooker. In a small bowl, combine tomato sauce and Worcestershire sauce and mix well. Pour over the chicken and vegetables in the slow cooker; stir gently to combine. Cover and cook on low for 7 hours. Stir in the beans and corn. Now cover and cook on low for an additional 30 minutes. To serve, remove bones from the chicken thighs. Stir chicken into stew mixture; mix well. Enjoy!

Chicken Casablanca

Ingredients

2 tbsp.. Olive oil
2 large Onions,, slice
1 tsp. tsp. Fresh ginger, grate
3 cloves garlic,, mince
3 pounds boneless skinless chicken breasts
3 large Carrots,, dice
2 large Potatoes, peel and, dice

2 tbsp.. Raisins
½ tsp. tsp. Cumin
½ tsp. tsp. Turmeric
½ tsp. tsp. Salt and pepper
¼ tsp. tsp. Cinnamon
¼ tsp. tsp. Cayenne pepper
1 Can chopped tomatoes,, (14 1/2 ounces)

3 medium Zucchini,, 1" slice   2 tbsp.. Parsley,, chopped
1 Can garbanzo beans,, (15 ounces) drain   ½ tsp. tsp. Cilantro

Method

Sauté the onions, ginger and garlic in oil. Transfer to crock pot. Cook brown chicken in same pan over medium heat. Now add the carrots, potatoes and zucchini to crock pot. Place the chicken on top of veggies. Stir seasonings in a small brown and sprinkle over chicken. Add raisins and tomatoes. Cover and cook on HIGH for 4 to 6 hours. Add the beans, parsley and cilantro 30 minutes before serving. Serve over cooked rice or couscous. Enjoy!

Chicken Cordon Bleu

Ingredients

4-6 chicken breasts (pounded out thin) •   1 can cream of mushroom soup (can use
4-6 pieces of ham •   any cream soup) •
4-6 slices of Swiss or mozzarella cheese • ¼ cup milk

Method

Put the ham and cheese on chicken. Roll up and secure with a toothpick. Place the chicken in the crock pot so it looks like a triangle layer the rest on top. Mix soup with the milk and pour over the chicken. Cover and cook on low for 4 hours or until chicken is no longer pink. Serve over noodles with the sauce. Enjoy!

Chicken Dinner in A Crock-Pot

Ingredients

4 skinless boneless chicken breasts
2 tsp. dried basil
1/8 tsp. salt and pepper
1 cup diced bell pepper
1 (16-oz.) can white beans, drained and rinsed
1 (14-oz.) can tomatoes, undrained

Method

Place the chicken in a crock pot, sprinkle with basil and salt and pepper. Add bell pepper, beans and tomatoes. Cover with the lid; cook on low setting for 8 hours. Serving size is 1 chicken breast with 1 cup of tomato bean mixture. Enjoy!

Chicken In Mushroom Gravy

Ingredients

6 Whole boneless skinless chicken breasts
21 ½ ounces 98% fat-free Condensed cream of Mushroom Soup
To taste Salt and Pepper
8 Oz Mushrooms, canned,, sliced and drained
½ Cup Dry White Wine

Method

Place the chicken breasts in the slow cooker. Season with salt and pepper. Mix the wine and the soup. Pour over the chicken. Add the mushrooms. Cover and Cook on LOW for 7 to 9 hours. Enjoy!

Chicken Italiano

Ingredients

1 pound boneless, skinless chicken thighs
1 medium onion,, chopped
½ cup pitted ripe olives,, halved
2 tbsp.. Capers1 tsp. tsp. dried oregano leaves
½ tsp. tsp. salt

½ tsp. tsp. dried rosemary leaves, crushed
¼ tsp. tsp. garlic powder
2 cups canned diced tomatoes,, undrained
¼ cup water
1 tbsp. cornstarch

Method

Place the chicken an in 3-1/2 to 4-quart slow cooker. Top with the onion, olives and capers. Sprinkle with oregano, salt, rosemary and garlic powder. Pour tomatoes over the chicken. Cover and cook on low setting for 7 to 10 hours or until chicken is fork-tender, its juices run clear and onion is tender. Remove the chicken and vegetables from a slow cooker with slotted spoon; place on serving platter. Cover to warm. In a small bowl, combine water and cornstarch; blend well. Add to a slow cooker. Increase setting to high; cook until thickened. Serve with chicken. Enjoy!

Chicken Paella

Ingredients

1 lb. Tyson boneless, skinless chicken thighs, or similar product (four 4-oz thighs)
2 medium tomatoes, chopped
1 medium onions, chopped
1 medium green pepper, chopped

1/2 cup chicken broth
3 medium garlic clove, chopped
1 tsp. dried oregano
1 tsp. ground turmeric
1/3 cup frozen green peas
2 cups cooked white rice

Method

Place the chicken, tomatoes, onion, pepper, broth, garlic, oregano and turmeric in a 4-quart or larger slow cooker (crock pot). Cover and cook on low setting for 5 hours. Add peas and rice; cook, uncovered, until peas are tender, about 15 minutes. Enjoy!

Chicken Parmesan

Ingredients

2 tsp. olive oil
4 skinless, boneless chicken breasts (about 3 oz.) each
1 ¼ cups crushed tomatoes
2 large cloves garlic, crushed
1 tsp. Sugar
Pinch of celery seeds
2 tbsp. dry red wine
½ cup shredded mozzarella cheese
2 tbsp. grated Parmesan cheese

Method

Heat the oil in a non-stick skillet over medium-high heat. Add the chicken and sauté, stirring occasionally, until lightly browned, about 10 min. Combine the chicken and next 5 ingredients in the crockery pot. Cover and cook on LOW until the chicken is cooked through and a meat thermometers registers 170 degrees F. Combine the cheeses in a small bowl and sprinkle them over the chicken. Don't stir. Cook until the cheeses are melted, about 15 min. Serve hot. Enjoy!

Chicken Stew

Ingredients

1 pound skinned, boneless chicken breasts
1 pound skinned, boneless chicken thighs
2 cups water
1 cup frozen small whole onions
1 cup sliced celery,, (1/2-inch)
1 cup thinly sliced carrots
1 tsp. tsp. paprika
½ tsp. tsp. salt
½ tsp. tsp. rubbed sage
½ tsp. tsp. dried thyme

½ tsp. tsp. pepper
1 (10-Ounce) can tomatoes and chilies
1 (14 1/4-ounce) can fat-free chicken broth
2 cups halved mushrooms
1 (6-ounce) can tomato paste
¼ cup water
3 tbsp.. cornstarch
2 cups frozen green peas

Method

Combine the first 15 ingredients in a large electric slow cooker. Cover with lid, and cook on high-heat setting for 4 hours or until carrot is tender. Combine water and cornstarch in a small bowl, stirring with a wire whisk until blended. Add cornstarch mixture and peas to slow cooker; stir well. Cover and cook on high-heat setting an additional 30 minutes. Enjoy!

Chicken Stroganoff

Ingredients

1 pound frozen boneless skinless chicken breasts
1 can fat free cream of mushroom soup
16-oz. carton fat free sour cream
1 envelope dry onion soup mix

Method

Put the frozen chicken in bottom of crock pot. Mix the soup, sour cream, onion soup mix and pour over chicken. Now cook on low for 7 hours. Make 6 servings. Enjoy!

Chicken Stroganoff #2

Ingredients

1 cup fat-free sour cream
1 tbsp. Gold Metal all-purpose flour

1 envelope chicken gravy mix, (.87 to 1.2 oz.)

1 cup water
1 pound boneless and skinless chicken breast,, cut into 1" pieces
16 ounces frozen California-blend vegetables, thawed
1 cup sliced mushroom, sautéed
1 cup frozen peas

10 ounces potatoes,, peeled cut into 1" pieces (approximate 2 potatoes, weight after peeled)
1 ½ cups Bisquick baking mix
4 green onions,, chopped (1/3 cups)
½ cup 1% low-fat milk

Method

Mix the sour cream, flour, gravy mix and water in a 3-1/2 to 4-quart Crock-Pot slow cooker until smooth. Stir in the chicken, vegetables and mushrooms. Cover and cook on low heat setting 4 hours or until chicken is tender and sauce is thickened. Stir in peas. Mix the baking mix and onions. Stir in milk just until moistened. Drop dough by rounded tablespoonfuls onto chicken and vegetables mixtures. Cover and cook on high heat setting 45 to 50 minutes or until toothpick inserted in center of dumplings coming out clean. Serve immediately, Enjoy!

Chicken Stroganoff Supreme

Ingredients

1 cup fat-free sour cream
1 tbsp. all-purpose flour
1 envelope chicken gravy mix
1 cup water
1 lb. boneless skinless chicken breast halves,, cut in 1" pieces

16 ounces frozen stew vegetables,, thawed
4 ounces mushroom pieces,, drained
1 cup frozen green peas,, thawed
1 ½ cups Bisquick and baking mix
4 whole green onions
½ cup skim milk

Method

Mix the sour cream, all-purpose flour, gravy mix and water in a 3 1/2 to 4-quart slow cooker until smooth. Stir in the chicken, stew vegetables and mushrooms. Cover and cook on Low heat setting for 5 hours or until chicken is tender and sauce is thickened. Stir in peas. Mix the baking mix and green onions. Stir in milk just until moistened. Drop dough by rounded tablespoonfuls onto chicken-vegetable mixture. Cover and cook on High heat setting for 45-50 minutes or until toothpick inserted in center of dumplings comes out clean. Serve immediately. Enjoy!

Chicken Wings in BBQ Sauce

Ingredients

3 pounds chicken wings,, about 16 wings
Salt and pepper, to taste
1 ½ cups barbecue sauce,, any variety
¼ cup honey
2 tsp. prepared mustard, or spicy mustard
2 tsp. Worcestershire sauce
Hot pepper sauce, to taste, optional

Method

Rinse the chicken and pat dry. Cut off and discard the wing tips. Cut each wing at the joint to make two sections. Place the wing parts on broiler pan. Broil 4 to 5 inches room heat 20 minutes, 10 minutes a side or until chicken is brown. Transfer the chicken to a Crock-Pot. For sauce, combine the barbecue sauce, honey, mustard, Worcestershire sauce, and hot pepper sauce, if desired, in a small bowl. Pour over the chicken wings. Cover and cook on Low 4 to 5 hours or on High 2 to 2 1/2 hours. Serve directly from Crock-Pot. Enjoy!

Chicken Wings in Honey Sauce

Ingredients

3 pounds chicken wings,, about 16 wings
Salt and pepper, to taste
2 cups honey
1 cup low sodium soy sauce
½ cup ketchup
¼ cup oil
Sesame seeds, optional

Method

Rinse the chicken and pat dry. Cut off and discard the wing tips. Cut each wing at joint to make two sections. Place the wing parts on broiler pan. Broil 4 to 5 inches from heat 20 minutes, 10 minutes a side or until the chicken is brown. Transfer the chicken to a Crock-Pot Slow Cooker. For sauce, combine honey, soy sauce, ketchup, oil and garlic in bowl. Pour over the chicken wings. Cover and cook on Low 4 to 5 hours or on High 2 to 2 1/2 hours. Garnish with sesame seeds, if desired. Enjoy!

Chicken Wings in Teriyaki Sauce

Ingredients

3 pounds chicken wings,, about 16 wings
1 large onion, chopped
1 cup brown sugar
1 cup low sodium soy sauce
¼ cup dry sherry, or chicken broth
2 tsp. ground ginger
2 cloves garlic, minced

Method

Rinse the chicken and pat dry. Cut off and discard the wing tips. Cut each wing at joint to make two sections. Place the wing parts on broiler pan. Broil 4 to 5 inches from heat 20 minutes, 10 minutes a side or until chicken is brown. Transfer the chicken to Crock-Pot Slow Cooker. Now mix the onion, brown sugar, soy sauce, cooking sherry (or chicken broth), ginger and garlic together in a bowl. Pour over the chicken wings. Cover and cook on Low 5 to 6 hours or on High 2 to 3 hours. Stir the chicken wings once to ensure wings are evenly coated with sauce. Serve from Crock-Pot Slow Cooker. Enjoy!

Chicken with Lima Beans

Ingredients

1 whole Frying chicken,, cut up
To taste Salt
To taste Pepper
1 tbsp. Oil
2 large Potatoes,, cubed
1 package frozen lima beans, thawed
1 cup Chicken broth
¼ tsp. tsp. thyme

Method

Season the chicken with salt and pepper. Heat the oil and butter in large skillet. Fry the chicken on both sides until brown. Add to a crock pot with the remaining ingredients. Cover and cook on low for 4 to 6 hours. Enjoy!

Chili

Ingredients

1 Pound Ground Sirloin
2 Cans kidney beans
1 Large Can tomato juice, low sodium,
1 Small Head cabbage,, sliced
1 Medium onion,, chopped
1 Small Can Tomato,, chopped
1 Pinch salt,
1 Tsp. tsp. chili powder, (1 to 2)

Method

This can be cooked on the stove or in a crock pot. Put tomato juice in the pot or crockpot. Now, brown ground beef and add to the juice. You can now add the rest of the ingredients. Cook over simmer heat until the cabbage is done or to the consistency, you like. Stir occasionally. You can serve this over rice and you can also sprinkle with cheese. It is really good. Enjoy!

Chili Mac Pot

Ingredients

16 ounces extra lean ground turkey or beef
1 cup chopped onion
2 cups (one 16 ounce can) tomatoes,
2 cups coarsely chopped
2 cups undrained
1 (10 3/4 ounce) can Healthy Request Tomato Soup
1 cup reduced-sodium tomato juice
2 tsp. chili seasoning
6 ounces (one 8 ounce can) red kidney beans, rinsed and drained
1 cup elbow macaroni

Method

In a large skillet sprayed with the olive oil flavored cooking spray, brown meat. Meanwhile, in a slow cooker container sprayed with cooking spray, combine the onion, undrained tomatoes, tomato soup, tomato juice, and chili seasoning. Stir in kidney beans and uncooked macaroni. Add browned meat. Mix well to combine. Cover and cook on LOW for 6 to 8 hours. Mix well before serving. Enjoy!

Chili Pasta Bake

Ingredients

1 ½ lbs. lean ground beef
1 cup chopped onion
2 (14 oz.) cans tomatoes with juice, mashed
2 tsp. chili powder
½ tsp. dried whole oregano

7.5 oz. tomato juice
1 tsp. Salt
¼ tsp. Pepper
1 ¼ cups uncooked elbow macaroni
1 cup grated Monterrey Jack (or medium Cheddar) cheese

Method

Scramble fry ground beef in a nonstick frying pan until browned. Drain well. Transfer to 3 1/2 quart slow cooker. Add the next 8 ingredients and stir. Cover and cook on low for 5 to 7 hours or on HIGH for 2 ½ to 3 ½ hours. Sprinkle cheese over top. Cook on HIGH for 10-15 min. until cheese is melted. Serve hot. Enjoy!

Chunky Beef and Pork Chili

Ingredients

1 pound beef round steak
1 pound pork shoulder steak
1 large onion,, chopped (1 cup)
2 cloves garlic,, finely chopped
15 ounces chunky tomato sauce
12 ounces thick-and-chunky salsa

2 tsp. Mexican seasoning*
1 medium green bell pepper,, chopped (1 cup)
sour cream,
cheddar cheese,, shredded

Method

Remove excess fat from the beef and pork. Cut the beef and pork into 3/4" pieces. Mix beef, pork and the remaining ingredients except bell pepper, sour cream and cheese in a 3 1/2 to 6 quart slow cooker. Cover and cook on low heat setting 8 to 10 hours or until the pork is tender. Stir in bell pepper. Cover and cook on low heat setting 15 to 30 minutes or until bell pepper is tender. Serve chili topped with sour cream and cheese if desired. Enjoy!

Cola-chicken

Ingredients

1 cup Cola,, regular

1 cup ketchup
1 whole Onion,, sliced
1 ½ pounds boneless skinless chicken breast

Method

Wash and pat the dry chicken. Now add salt and pepper to taste. Put the chicken in a crock pot and add onions on top. Add cola and Ketchup and cook on LOW 6 to 8 hours. When cooked place in refrigerator to cool and then skim off the fat. Reheat and eat. Enjoy!

Comforting Crock Pot Chili

Ingredients

1 pound ground turkey breast or very lean ground beef
1 large onion,, finely chopped
5 oz. pinto beans,, rinsed and drained
8.5 oz. corn, rinsed and drained
15 oz. tomato sauce

14 ½ oz. diced tomatoes
10 oz. diced tomato and green chilies
1 tbsp. chili powder
1 tsp. ground cumin
½ tsp. garlic powder
½ tsp. salt

Method

In a nonstick skillet over medium heat, cook ground meat until meat is no longer pink; drain. Transfer meat to Crock Pot. Add remaining ingredients and stir until combined. Cook on high heat for 4 hours; remove lid and stir quickly halfway through. Serve hot. Enjoy!

Country Captain Chicken with Rice

Ingredients

2 cups sliced shiitake mushrooms
1 cup chopped onion
½ cup chopped celery
1 clove garlic, minced
1 lb. (450g) boneless, skinless chicken thighs, trimmed of all fat and cut into bite-size pieces
1 tbsp. Flour
¼ cup fat-free chicken broth
1 ½ tsp. curry powder

1 tsp. Salt
¼ tsp. Pepper
¼ tsp. Paprika
3 cups canned crushed tomatoes
¼ cup golden raisins
2 cups cooked brown rice

Method

Coat a large skillet with the cooking spray. Add the mushrooms, onion, celery and garlic and sauté until vegetables are tender, about 5 minutes. Place the vegetables in a slow cooker; add the chicken. In a cup, stir together flour and chicken broth until smooth and add to slow cooker. Add curry powder, salt, pepper, paprika, crushed tomatoes and raisins, and stir in. Cover and cook on low for 5 hours. To serve, spoon 1/2 cup rice onto each 4 plates. Top each with chicken and sauce and serve. Enjoy!

Cowboy Stew

Ingredients

1 ¼ lbs. beef stew meat
4 potatoes, unpeeled, cut into 4" pcs.
½ cup onion, chopped
1 tsp. salt
¼ tsp. pepper
1 (28 oz.) can Baked beans in BBQ Sauce

Method

Mix the beef, potatoes, onion, salt and pepper in a 3 1/2 to 4 quart slow cooker. Spread beans over the beef mixture. Cover and cook on LOW 8-10 hours or until beef is tender. Enjoy!

Cozy Crock Comfort

Ingredients

16 oz. ground 90% lean turkey or beef
½ cup chopped onion
3 cups (15 oz.) diced raw potatoes
1/3 cup (1 oz.) uncooked regular rice
1 ½ cups shredded carrots
1 cup finely diced celery

1 ½ cups Healthy Request Tomato Juice or any reduced-sodium Tomato juice
1 (10 3/4 oz.) can Healthy Request Tomato Soup
¼ tsp. black pepper
1 tsp. dried parsley flakes

Method

In a large skillet sprayed with butter flavored spray, add brown meat. Place browned meat in a slow cooker container. Add the onion, potatoes, uncooked rice, carrots and celery. Mix well to combine. Stir in tomato juice, tomato soup, black pepper and parsley flakes. Cover and cook on LOW for 6 to 8 hours. Mix well before serving. Enjoy!

Creamy Chicken and Wild Rice

Ingredients

1 package (8.25 oz.) skillet-dinner mix for mushroom and wild rice
1 lb. skinless, boneless chicken breast, cut into 1 piece
1 can (14 1/2 oz.) ready-to-serve chicken broth
1 can (12 oz.) evaporated milk
½ cup water
2 tbsp. margarine or butter, melted
2 tbsp. instant chopped onion

Method

Mix the uncooked rice and sauce mix (from dinner mix) and add the remaining ingredients in 2-3 1/2 quart slow cooker. Cover and cook on LOW 5 to 6 hours, or until rice is tender. Stir mixture. Cover and let stand about 15 minutes or until thickened and desired consistency. Enjoy!

Crockpot Baked Beans

Ingredients

½ medium onion,, chopped
5 slices turkey bacon,, chopped
4 ounces ground beef (80% lean)
1 can vegetarian beans in tomato sauce, (16 oz.)
1 can vegetarian baked beans, (16 oz.)
1 can red kidney beans, (16 oz.),, rinsed, drained
½ cup tomato sauce
2 tbsp.. brown sugar
1 tsp. tsp. liquid smoke,
½ tsp. tsp. maple flavoring

Method

Lightly spray an unheated medium skillet with non-stick spray. Add the onions and bacon. Cook and stir over medium-high heat until the onions are tender. Add the ground beef and cook until browned, stirring occasionally. Transfer the onion mixture to a 4 to 6-quart crock pot. Stir in the beans in tomato sauce, baked beans, kidney beans, tomato sauce, brown sugar, liquid smoke and maple flavoring. Cover and cook on the medium-high heat setting for 4 to 6 hours (if necessary, adjust the heat setting so the beans slowly simmer during cooking). Stir before serving. Enjoy!

Crockpot Beef and Peppers

Ingredients

2 lb. lean round steak, trim all fat
2 green peppers, sliced thin
2 tbsp. dried onions, 1 used two large fresh onions
1 cup beef broth
2 tbsp. low sodium soy sauce
1 tsp. Worcestershire sauce
½ tsp. ground ginger
1 clove garlic, minced

Method

Cut the steak into serving size pieces. Put the vegetables in the bottom of the crock pot, now put the steak in a single layer on top of the vegetables. Pour the rest of the ingredients over the top. Cover and cook on low 8-10 hours or high for about 4 hours. Enjoy!

Crockpot Beef Stew

Ingredients

3 potatoes, diced
5 carrots, diced
4 stalks celery, diced
2 small onions, chopped
1 head (not clove) garlic, minced
1 large tomato, blanched and chopped
4 tbsp. barley
4 beef bouillon cubes
1 ¾ pounds lean beef
½ tsp. rosemary
½ tsp. savory
1 tsp. salt
½ tsp. pepper
2 tbsp. flour
2 tbsp. corn starch

Method

Cube and brown the beef. Add flour to beef and stir together. Combine all ingredients except potatoes, corn starch, rosemary, and savory in a crock pot. Cover with water. Cook on high 12-24 hours. 1 hour before serving, add the potatoes, rosemary, and savory. Immediately before serving, thicken with corn starch. Enjoy!

Crockpot Company Chicken Casserole

Ingredients

8 ounces noodles
3 cups boneless skinless chicken breasts,, cooked, diced
½ cup celery,, diced
½ cup green pepper,, diced
½ cup onion,, diced
4 ounces mushrooms,, canned and drained

½ cup non-fat chicken broth
½ cup fat-free Parmesan cheese
1 can cream of chicken soup,, melted
1 cup sharp cheddar cheese,, grated
½ tsp. tsp. basil
1 ½ cups low fat cottage cheese,, small curd
2 ½ cups water

Method

Cook the noodles according to package directions until barely tender; drain and rinse thoroughly. In a large bowl, combine the remaining ingredients with the noodles, making sure the noodles are separated and coated with liquid. Pour mixture into a greased crock pot. Cover and cook on LOW for 6 to 10 hours. Now cook on HIGH for 3-4 hours. Serve hot. Enjoy!

Crockpot Creamy Chicken Fettuccine

Ingredients

1 ½ pounds boneless skinless chicken breasts, cut into cubes
½ tsp. tsp. garlic powder
½ tsp. tsp. onion powder
1/8 tsp. tsp. pepper
1 10-3/4 ounce can condensed cream of chicken soup, undiluted
1 10-3/4 ounce can condensed cream of celery soup, undiluted

4 ounces process American cheese, cubed
1 2-1/4 ounce can sliced ripe olives, drained
1 2 ounce jar diced pimientos,, drained, optional
1 16 ounce package spinach fettuccine or spaghetti
Thin bread sticks

Method

Place the chicken in a slow cooker; sprinkle with garlic powder, onion powder and pepper. Top with soups. Cover and cook on high for 3-4 hours or until chicken juices run clear. Stir in cheese, olives and pimientos if desired. Cover and cook until cheese is melted. Meanwhile, cook fettuccine according to package directions; drain. Serve with the chicken and bread sticks if desired. Enjoy!

Crockpot Easy French Dip Sandwiches

Ingredients

3 pounds fresh beef brisket (not corned beef)
1 (1.3 oz.) package dry onion soup mix
1 (10.5 oz.) can condensed beef broth
8 mini baguettes or sandwich buns

Method

Place beef in a 3 1/2 to 6 quart slow cooker. Mix the dry soup mix and beef broth; pour over beef. Cover and cook on low heat setting 8 to 10 hours or until beef is tender. Skim fat from liquid. Remove beef; cut across grain into thin slices. Cut each baguette horizontally in half. Fill baguettes with beef; cut in half. Serve with broth for dipping. Enjoy!

Crockpot Family Favorite Pot Roast

Ingredients

2 ½ pounds beef bottom round roast
2 tsp. olive or vegetable oil
3 medium potatoes,, cut into 2" pieces
2 ½ cups baby-cut carrots
2 cups sliced mushrooms
1 medium stalk celery,, sliced
1 medium onion,, chopped
1 tsp. tsp. salt
½ tsp. tsp. pepper
½ tsp. tsp. dried thyme leaves
1 (14.5 oz.) can diced tomatoes,, undrained
1 (10.5 oz.) can condensed beef consommé or broth
1 (5.5 oz.) can eight-vegetable juice
¼ cup Gold Medal all-purpose flour

Method

Remove excess fat from beef. Heat oil in 10-inch skillet over medium-high heat. Cook beef in oil about 10 minutes, turning occasionally; until brown on all sides. Place potatoes, carrots, mushrooms, celery and onion in 4 to 5 quart slow cooker. Sprinkle with salt, pepper and thyme. Place beef on vegetables. Pour tomatoes, consommé and vegetable juice over beef. Cover and cook on low heat setting 8 to 10 hours or until beef and vegetables are tender. Remove beef and vegetables from slow cooker, using slotted spoon; place on serving platter and keep warm. Skim fat from beef juices in slow cooker if desired. Remove 1/2 cup of the juices from the slow cooker; mix with flour until smooth using wire whisk. Gradually stir flour mixture into remaining juices in slow cooker. Cook on high heat setting about 15 minutes or until thickened. Serve sauce with beef and vegetables. Enjoy!

Crockpot Green Chili Chicken Stew

Ingredients

5 whole boned and skinned chicken breast halves, cut in 1" cubes
1 ¼ tsp. ground cumin
1 Tsp. tsp. dried sage
2 Large onions,, chopped
2 Cloves garlic,, minced
1 tbsp. cider vinegar
6 Small red potatoes,, quartered
3 whole poblano peppers,, seeded and diced
10 tomatillos,, husked, chopped
1 ½ Cups fat-free chicken broth
½ Cup chopped cilantro

Method

The original recipe called for 2 pounds of beef round or chuck, cut in 1 inch pieces, but I substituted 5 boneless, skinless chicken breast halves, and it turned out fine. Combine all the ingredients except cilantro in crock pot. Cover and cook on low setting for 8-10 hours. Serve garnished with chopped cilantro. Enjoy!

Crockpot Ham and Lima Beans

Ingredients

1 pound dry lima beans, soaked overnight
1 whole chopped onion
1 whole green pepper,, chopped
1 tsp. tsp. dry mustard
1 tsp. tsp. salt
1 tsp. tsp. pepper
¼ pound extra lean ham or bacon (up to 1/2 lb.),, cut in small pieces
1 cup water
1 can tomato soup

Method

Put all the ingredients in crock-pot and stir well. Cover and cook on low for 7 to 10 hours, high 4 to 5 hours. Serve with hot corn bread. Enjoy!

Crockpot Home-Style Turkey Dinner

Ingredients

3 medium Yukon gold potatoes, cut into 2" pieces
3 turkey thighs,, skin removed
1 (12-oz) jar home-style turkey gravy
2 tbsp.. Gold Medal all-purpose flour
1 tsp. tsp. parsley flakes
½ tsp. tsp. dried thyme leaves
1/8 tsp. tsp. pepper
1 lb. bag frozen baby bean and carrot blend, thawed and drained

Method

Place the potatoes in a 3 1/2 to 6 quart slow cooker; arrange turkey on top. Mix the remaining ingredients except vegetables until smooth; pour over mixture in slow cooker. Cover and cook on low heat setting 8 to 10 hours or until juice of turkey is no longer pink when centers of thickest pieces are cut. Stir in vegetables. Cover and cook on low heat setting about 30 minutes or until vegetables are tender. Remove turkey and vegetables from slow cooker, using slotted spoon. Stir sauce; serve with turkey and vegetables. Enjoy!

Crockpot Italian Chicken

Ingredients

4 Whole Boneless Skinless Chicken Breast Halves
16 ounces tomatoes,, (or 2-3 fresh tomatoes)
1 Whole onion,, sliced
1 Tsp. tsp. Italian seasoning
1 Whole Green Bell Pepper,, seeded and chopped
Salt And Pepper, to taste

Method

Mix all the ingredients in the crock pot and cook on low 8-10 hours. Serve hot. Enjoy!

Crockpot Italian Chicken #2

Ingredients

3 lb. frozen boneless, skinless chicken breast (thawed)

1 envelope Good Seasons Italian Dressing (dry not made) I used their low-fat one
1 envelope Onion Soup Mix (dry not made)
1 tsp. garlic or minced garlic (I used fresh)
1 jar pepperoni Mild or Hot (your choice)

Method

Put all the chicken in a crock pot sprayed with Pam. In a bowl mix the remaining ingredients (with pepperoncini juice and all) together, be careful not to break up the peppers. Pour all over the chicken and cook for 8 to 9 hours on low. No peeking. When done pick out the peppers and put in a serving dish to use on sandwiches for those who like hotter sandwiches. Use a sturdy spoon and break apart the chicken, it is very tender. Serve 1/2 cup on a Healthy Lite bun and the whole sandwich . Drain off most of the juices, add BBQ sauce for great BBQ sandwiches the next day. Freeze in little containers to have in a pinch. Enjoy!

Crockpot Lemon Chicken

Ingredients

6 whole boneless skinless chicken breasts
½ cup all-purpose flour
1 tsp. tsp. salt
1 tbsp. balsamic vinegar
3 tbsp.. ketchup
3 tbsp.. brown sugar
6 oz. frozen lemonade concentrate
2 tbsp.. cornstarch
¼ cup water

Method

Dredge the chicken in flour mixed with salt. Shake off excess and brown in a hot skillet. Remove the chicken and put in the crock pot. Mix the lemonade, brown sugar, vinegar (use regular vinegar if you prefer) and ketchup and pour over the chicken. Cook on high for 3-4 hours. When ready to serve, remove the chicken to a warm platter and thicken the sauce with the cornstarch/water solution, and serve along with the chicken. Enjoy!

Crockpot Meatloaf Recipe

Ingredients

1 lb. extra lean ground beef
1 lb. ground turkey
2 cups soft breadcrumbs
½ cup Marinara sauce
1 whole egg
2 tbsp. Dried Onion, chopped
1 ¼ tsp. tsp. salt
1 Tsp. tsp. Garlic Salt
½ tsp. tsp. dried Italian seasoning...crushed
¼ tsp. tsp. Garlic Powder
¼ tsp. tsp. pepper
2 tbsp. Marinara Sauce

Method

Fold a 30-inch long piece of foil in half lengthwise. Place it in the bottom of a slow cooker with both ends hanging over the top edge of cooker. In a large bowl, mix the ground beef, ground turkey, bread crumbs, 1/2 cup marinara sauce, egg, onion, salt, garlic salt, Italian herbs, garlic powder and pepper until well blended. Shape the mixture into a loaf. Place in slow cooker on top of foil. Spread 2 tbsp. marinara sauce over top. Cover tightly and cook on LOW for 5 to 6 Hours or on HIGH for 2 1/2 to 3 hours. Use ends of foil to lift out meat loaf and transfer to a serving platter. Enjoy!

Crockpot Mexican Pork

Ingredients

1 pound pork boneless loin roast, cut into 1" pieces
1 (20 oz.) jar salsa
1 (4 oz.) can chopped green chilies,, drained
1 (15 oz.) can black beans,, rinsed and drained
1 cup shredded Monterrey jack cheese,, if desired

Method

Mix the pork, salsa and chilies in a 3 1/2 to 4 quart slow cooker. Cover and cook on low heat setting 6 to 8 hour or until pork is tender. Stir in beans. Cover and cook about 5 minutes or until hot. Sprinkle with cheese. Enjoy!

Crockpot Multi-Bean Soup

Ingredients

5 (14.5oz) cans chicken or vegetable broth
1 (20 oz.) package 15 or 16 dried bean soup mix,, sorted and rinsed
4 medium carrots,, chopped
3 medium stalks celery,, chopped

1 large onion,, chopped
2 tbsp.. tomato paste
1 tsp. tsp. salt
1 tsp. tsp. Italian seasoning
½ tsp. tsp. pepper
1 (14.5oz) can diced tomatoes,, drained

Method

Mix all the ingredients except tomatoes in a 5 to 6 quart slow cooker. Cover and cook on low heat setting 8 to 10 hours or until beans are tender. Stir in tomatoes. Cover and cook on high heat setting about 15 minutes or until hot. Enjoy!

Crockpot Pork Chop Supper

Ingredients

6 pork loin or rib chops,, 1/2 inch thick
6 medium new potatoes,, cut into eighths
1 (10.75 oz.) can condensed cream of mushroom soup
1 (4 oz.) can mushroom pieces and stems,, drained
2 tbsp.. dry white wine

¼ tsp. tsp. dried thyme leaves
½ tsp. tsp. garlic powder
½ tsp. tsp. Worcestershire sauce
3 tbsp.. Gold Medal all-purpose flour
1 tbsp. diced pimientos
1 (10 oz.) package frozen green peas,, rinsed and drained

Method

Spray a 10-inch nonstick skillet with cooking spray; heat over medium-high heat. Cook the pork a in skillet, turning once, until brown. Place potatoes in a 3 ½ to 6 quart slow cooker. Mix the soup, mushrooms, wine, thyme, garlic powder, Worcestershire sauce and flour; spoon half of soup mixture over the potatoes. Place the pork on potatoes, cover with the remaining soup mixture. Cover and cook on low heat setting 6 to 7 hours or until the pork is tender. Remove the pork; keep warm. Stir pimientos and peas into a slow cooker. Cover and cook on low heat setting about 15 minutes or until peas are tender. Serve with pork. Enjoy!

Crockpot Potato Chowder

Ingredients

2 cups potatoes, cut into 1/2-inch cubes
1 large carrot, diced
1 cup chopped leek, white part only
1 clove garlic, minced
4 cups fat-free chicken broth
½ cups pearl barley
1 bay leaf

¼ tsp. dried, crushed thyme
¼ tsp. pepper
4 oz. Canadian bacon, cut into 1/4-inch pieces
½ cup evaporated fat-free milk
¼ cup fat-free half-and-half

Method

In a slow cooker, combine the potatoes, carrots, leek, garlic, chicken broth, barley, bay leaf, thyme, pepper, and Canadian bacon. Cover and cook on low for 6 hours or until the vegetables and barley are tender. Stir in evaporated milk and half-and half and heat through, uncovered, about 10 minutes. Enjoy!

Crockpot Pulled-Pork Fajitas

Ingredients

½ pound pork boneless loin roast
1 medium onion,, thinly sliced
2 cups barbecue sauce
¾ cup salsa
3 tbsp.. chili powder
1 tbsp. Mexican seasoning
9 flour tortillas

Method

Remove excess fat from the pork. Place the pork in a 3 1/2 to 6 quart slow cooker; arrange onion on top. Mix the remaining ingredients except tortillas; pour over the pork. Cover and cook on low heat setting 8 to 10 hours or until the pork is very tender. Remove the pork; place on a large plate. Use 2 forks to pull the pork into shreds. Pour sauce into a bowl; stir in the pork. Spoon filling onto tortillas; roll up and serve. Enjoy!

Crockpot Savory Chicken and Vegetables

Ingredients

8 boneless, skinless chicken thighs
2 cups chicken broth
1 tsp. tsp. salt
¼ tsp. tsp. pepper
8 ounces pearl onions
6 slices bacon,, cooked and crumbled
2 cloves garlic,, finely chopped
Bouquet Garni, (recipe given)1 lb. bag baby-cut carrots
1 pound small whole button mushrooms
2 tbsp.. Gold Medal all-purpose flour
2 tbsp.. cold water

Method

Place the chicken in a 5 to 6 quart slow cooker. Add the remaining ingredients except mushrooms, flour and water. Cover and cook on low heat setting 8 to 10 hours or until the juice of chicken is no longer pink when centers of thickest pieces are cut. Remove fat from the surface. Remove Bouquet Garni. Stir in mushrooms. Mix flour and water; stir into chicken mixture. Cover and cook on high heat setting 30 minutes or until thickened.
For Bouquet Garni: Tie 4 sprigs parsley, 2 bay leaves and 1 tsp. dried thyme leaves in cheesecloth bag or place in tea ball. Enjoy!

Italian Beef and Green Pepper Sandwiches

Ingredients

2 lb. fresh beef brisket
1 tbsp. vegetable oil
1 can (10 1/2 oz.) condensed beef broth
2 cloves garlic, finely chopped
1 tsp. dried oregano leaves
1 tsp. dried basil leaves
½ tsp. salt
¼ tsp. pepper
¼ tsp. crushed red pepper
2 medium green bell peppers, cut into1/4" strips
12 slices crusty Italian or French bread, each about 1" thick

Method

Trim excess fat from the beef. Heat the oil in a 10" skillet over medium-high heat. Cook the beef in oil about 10 min., turning occasionally, until both sides are brown. Place the beef in a 3 1/2 to 6 quart slow cooker. Mix the remaining ingredients except bell peppers and bread; pour over beef. Cover and cook on LOW 8-10 hours or until beef is tender. Remove the beef to cutting board; cut into thin slices. Skim fat from the beef juices in cooker. Stir bell peppers into juices. Cover and cook on HIGH 15 minutes and return the beef slices to cooker. Place 2 slices of bread on each plate. Spoon the beef mixture over bread. Enjoy!

Italian Bow Tie Supper

Ingredients

½ Pound Extra Lean Ground Beef,, browned and drained
1 Medium Onion, chopped
1 Clove Garlic, minced
8 Ounces Tomato Sauce
14 ½ Ounces Canned Tomatoes, stewed
1 Tsp. tsp. Dried Oregano
1 Tsp. tsp. Italian Seasoning

Salt And Pepper, to taste
8 Ounces Pasta,, cooked and drained
10 Ounces Frozen Spinach,, thawed and drained
1 Cup Mozzarella Cheese, Part Skim Milk, shredded
½ Cup Fat-free Parmesan Cheese, grated

Method

Place the all ingredients, except for cooked pasta, spinach and cheeses in a slow cooker. Cover and cook on low 7 to 8 hours or until bubbly. Increase the slow cooker to high; stir in pasta, spinach and cheeses. Cover and cook for 10 minutes or until heated through and cheeses are melted. Enjoy!

Italian Pot Roast

Ingredients

1 (2 1/2-pounds) boneless beef round roast
1 medium onion, sliced
¼ tsp. Salt
¼ tsp. Pepper
2 (8-ounce) cans no-salt-added tomato sauce
1 (0.7-ounce) package Italian salad dressing mix

Method

Slice the roast in half and place it in a 3 1/2 quart electric slow cooker. Add onion and the remaining ingredients. Cover and cook on high setting 5 hours or until the roast is tender. Or, cover and cook on high setting 1 hour; reduce to low setting and cook 7 hours. Slice meat to serve. Enjoy!

Italian Spaghetti Sauce

Ingredients

2 pounds extra lean ground beef or bulk Italian Sausage
3 medium chopped onions, (2-1/4 cups)
1 large green bell pepper,, chopped (1-1/2 cups)
6 cloves garlic,, finely chopped
29 ounces canned diced tomatoes,, undrained

29 ounces tomato sauce
12 ounces tomato paste
2 tbsp.. dried basil leaves
1 tbsp. oregano leaves
1 tbsp. sugar, or Splenda
1 tsp. tsp. salt
½ tsp. tsp. pepper
½ tsp. tsp. crushed red pepper

Method

Cook the ground beef (or sausage), onions, bell pepper and garlic in a 12-inch skillet over medium heat about 10 minutes, stirring occasionally, until the meat is no long pink; drain. Spoon the meat mixture into a 5 quart Crock-Pot slow cooker. Stir in the remaining ingredients. Cover and cook on low heat setting for 8 or 9 hours or until the vegetables are tender. Enjoy!

Italian Tortellini Stew

Ingredients

1 onion, chopped
2 zucchini, sliced
32-oz chicken broth
28-oz crushed tomatoes
15-oz great northern beans
2 tbsp. basil
¼ tsp. salt
¼ tsp. pepper
8 oz. dry cheese filled tortellini

Method

Combine all the ingredients, except tortellini, in a slow cooker container. Cook on low for 6 hours. Turn heat to high and add the tortellini. Cook for 20 minutes. Serve hot. Enjoy!

Italian Turkey Rice Dinner

Ingredients

3 medium carrots, shredded (2 cups)
2 medium stalks celery, sliced (1 cup)
1 small red bell pepper, chopped (1/2 cup)
½ tsp. dried basil leaves
1/3 cup water
4 turkey thighs (8-12 oz. each), skin removed

1 tsp. salt
¼ tsp. pepper
½ cup uncooked regular long-grain rice
1 tsp. dried oregano leaves
1/3 cup shredded Italian-style
6 cheese blend or mozzarella cheese (2 oz.)

Method

Mix the carrots, celery, bell pepper, basil and water in 3 1/2-4 quart slow cooker. Sprinkle the turkey with salt and pepper; place on the vegetable mixture. Cover and cook on LOW for 6 to 7 hours Remove the turkey thighs. Stir the rice and oregano into the vegetable mixture; return the turkey to slow cooker. Cover and cook on LOW about 1 hour or until the rice is tender. Remove the turkey thighs. Stir the cheese into rice mixture until melted. Serve with turkey. Enjoy!

Italian Turkey Dinner

Ingredients

2 (1 lb.) turkey thighs, skin removed
1 (14.5 oz.) can diced tomatoes with Italian-style herbs, undrained
2 tbsp. tomato paste
2 cloves garlic, minced
1 cup uncooked couscous
1 ½ cups water
2 cups sliced zucchini

Method

Place the turkey thighs in a 3 1/2-4 quart slow cooker. In small bowl, combine the tomatoes, tomato paste and garlic; mix well. Pour over the turkey. Cover and cook on LOW for 6-8 hours About 25 minutes before serving, cook the couscous in water as directed on the package. Stir zucchini into tomato mixture. Cover and cook on HIGH for an additional 20 minutes or until zucchini is tender. To serve, remove bones from the turkey. Stir gently to break up turkey and serve. Enjoy!

Jambalaya

Ingredients

1 cup diced lean boiled ham
2 onions, coarsely chopped
2 celery stalks, sliced
½ green bell pepper, seeded and chopped
1 (28-ounce) can whole tomatoes
¼ cup tomato paste
3 garlic cloves, minced

1 tbsp. chopped parsley
½ tsp. tsp. dried thyme
2 whole cloves
1 tbsp. vegetable oil
1 cup long-grain white rice
1 pound medium shrimp, peeled and deveined

Method

Combine the ham, onions, celery, bell pepper, tomatoes, tomato paste, garlic, parsley, thyme, cloves, oil, and rice in a slow cooker. Cook on High for 4-5 hours. Add the shrimp and cook until the shrimp are pink, about 1 hour longer. Enjoy!

Make-Ahead Fajitas

Ingredients

1 ½ lbs. beef flank steak, fat trimmed, cut into 32 strips
1 medium (1/2 cup) onion, sliced
1 small (1/2 cup) green pepper, sliced
1 small (1/2 cup) red pepper, sliced
1 (1 oz.) package fajita seasoning mix
1 tbsp. finely chopped fresh garlic
10 (8") flour tortillas, warmed
Toppings
Cheddar cheese, shredded, Low Fat sour cream, Salsa, Hot pepper sauce, Guacamole

Method

Stir together all filling ingredients in slow cooker. Cover; cook on LOW for 6-8 hrs., or HIGH 3, 4 hours Drain off liquid. Cut or shred meat, if desired. To serve, place meat mixture on warm tortillas. Top with desired toppings. Enjoy!

Mama's Chicken Stew

Ingredients

1 pound skinned, boned chicken breasts, cut into bite-size pieces
1 pound skinned, boned chicken thighs, cut into bite-size pieces
2 cups water
1 cup frozen small whole onions
1 cup (1/2-inch) sliced celery
1 cup thinly sliced carrot
1 tsp. paprika
½ tsp. salt
½ tsp. rubbed sage
½ tsp. dried thyme
½ tsp. black pepper
1 (14 ¼-ounce) can fat-free chicken broth
2 cups halved mushrooms
1 (6-ounce) can tomato paste
¼ cup water
3 tbsp.. cornstarch
2 cups frozen green peas

Method

Combine the first 14 ingredients in a large electric slow cooker. Cover with lid, and cook on high-heat setting for 4 hours or until the carrot is tender. Combine the water and cornstarch in a small bowl, stirring with a whisk until blended. Add the cornstarch mixture and peas to the slow cooker and stir well. Cover and cook on high-heat setting for an additional 30 minutes. Enjoy!

Mexi Dip

Ingredients

16 ounces light cream cheese, (2 8oz package)
6 ½ ounces canned flakes of ham, with liquid, mashed together
3 cups grated medium Cheddar cheese
½ cup Medium or hot Salsa
4 ounces canned chili peppers,, green, drained
½ tsp. tsp. chili powder,

Method

Mash the cream cheese with fork in a bowl. Spread it in the bottom of a3-1/2 quart slow cooker. Sprinkle ham evenly over top. Sprinkle with Cheddar cheese. Stir salsa and green chilies together. Spoon over the top. Sprinkle with chili powder. Cover and Cook on Low for 2 to 2-1/2 hours until quite warm. Do not stir. Enjoy!

Mexican Green Chili

Ingredients

1 ½ pounds lean top round, cut into 1 inch pieces

1 (16 ounce) jar tomatillo salsa (green salsa) (mild is advised)

1 (15 ounce) can Mexican style stewed tomatoes

1 (15 ounce) can fat-free beef broth

2 (4.5 ounce) cans chopped green chilies

1 cup chopped onion

2 tsp. ground cumin

1 tsp. tsp. freshly ground pepper

2 tsp. bottled minced garlic

2 tsp. chili oil

Method

Combine all the ingredients in an electric slow-cooker. Stir well. Cover and cook on low heat setting for 8 hours. Enjoy!

Mom's Homemade Chicken Soup

Ingredients

1 tbsp. vegetable oil

1 pound boneless skinless chicken breast halves,, cut into 1" pieces

1 medium stalk celery,, chopped (1/2 cup)

1 medium onion,, chopped (1/2 cup)

2 cloves garlic,, finely chopped

1 ½ cups baby carrots,, quartered

1 tbsp. chicken bouillon granules

1 tsp. tsp. dried thyme leaves

49 ½ ounces ready-to-serve chicken broth

1 cup frozen green peas

1 cup fine egg noodles

Method

Heat the oil in a 10-inch skillet over medium-high heat. Cook the chicken, stirring occasionally, until chicken is browned. Mix all the ingredients except peas and noodles in 3-1/2 to 4 quart Crock-Pot slow cooker. Cover and cook on low heat setting 6-1/2 to 7 hours or until the vegetables are tender and chicken is no longer pink in center. Rinse the frozen peas with cold water to separate and drain. Stir the peas and noodles into soup. Cover and cook on high heat setting about 15 minutes or until noodles are tender. Enjoy!

Mustard Onion Chuck Roast in Foil

Ingredients

8 servings borderline 6 or 7
2 tbsp. dry mustard
1 ½ tsp. Water

3 pound beef chuck pot roast
2 medium onions, chunked
½ cup soy sauce

Method

Blend the mustard and water to make a paste; let stand for 5 minutes. Place a large enough piece of foil to cover the meat in a shallow baking pan; place the meat on foil. Sprinkle onion pieces on meat. Stir 1 tablespoon soy sauce into mustard mixture, blending until smooth; stir in the remaining soy sauce. Pour mixture evenly over the beef and onions. Fold foil over meat; seal securely. Roast at 325 degrees for 3 hours. Remove from the oven, slice across grain, and serve with the meat juices. Cover and cook on low heat for 6 to 8 hours. Don't lift lid during cooking. Serve hot. Enjoy!

No-Peek Chicken Casserole

Ingredients

2 pounds boneless skinless chicken breasts,, (cut in 1" pieces)
1 envelope dry onion soup mix
1 can fat-free beef broth
1 can 98% fat-free cream of mushroom soup
4 ounces mushrooms,, drained

Method

Combine all the ingredients in crock pot. Stir together well. Cover and cook on low 8 to 12 hours or on high 3 to 4 hours. Serve over noodles or rice. Enjoy!

Peking Pork Chops

Ingredients

6 pork chops, about 1" thick
¼ cup brown sugar
1 tsp. ground ginger
½ cup soy sauce
¼ cup ketchup
1-2 cloves garlic, mashed

salt & pepper, to taste

Method

Trim excess fat from pork chops. Place pork chops in crockpot. Combine brown sugar, ground ginger, soy sauce, ketchup, garlic, salt & pepper. Pour mixture over meat in crockpot. Cover and cook on low for 4 to 6 hours, or until tender. Season with salt and pepper. Serve with steamed white rice or Chinese noodles. Enjoy!

Peles Hot Chicken Sandwich

Ingredients

1 lb. boneless, skinless chicken breasts, cut into 2 x 1/2-inch strips
1 red bell pepper, cut into julienne strips
6 mushrooms, sliced
¾ cup pineapple juice
2 tbsp. teriyaki sauce
1 tbsp. Honey
½ tsp. Salt
1/8 to ¼ tsp. dried red pepper flakes
2 tbsp. Cornstarch
2 tbsp. cold water
4-5 sesame bagels
1 small jicama, peeled and coarsely shredded

Method

Combine the first 9 ingredients in a 3 1/2 quart slow cooker. Cover and cook on LOW about 4 hours or until chicken is tender. Turn control to HIGH. In a small bowl, dissolve the cornstarch in cold water. Stir into contents of slow cooker. Cover and cook 15 to 20 minutes or until thickened. Meanwhile preheat the broiler. Split bagels and place, cut sides up, on a baking sheet. Toast under broiler until lightly browned, about 5 minutes. Serve the chicken mixture on bagels. Top with jicama. Enjoy!

Pepper Steak in the Crock

Ingredients

1 ½ pounds flank steak,, thinly sliced
1 large onion, sliced
2 bell peppers, any color, sliced
2 tbsp. soy sauce

2 tbsp. sesame oil
1 tablespoon brown sugar
3 cloves garlic, sliced

Method

Spray the crockpot with some pam spray. Place all the ingredients in the crock, mix well. Cook on low 8-9 hours. Serve hot. Enjoy!

Pepsi and Pork in the Crockpot

Ingredients

1 (10 oz.) can reduced-fat cream of mushroom soup
2 tbsp. reduced-sodium soy sauce
1 (12 oz.) can Diet Pepsi
4 (3 oz.) pork chops, trimmed well (or substitute with a pork roast)

Method

Mix the soup, soy sauce, and Diet Pepsi together at the bottom of the Crockpot. Place the chops in the mixture and cook on high medium or High for 4-6 hours. Serve hot. Enjoy!

Pineapple Chicken

Ingredients

3 Chicken breasts, split, skinned and boned
Pepper, to taste
Paprika, to taste

20 oz. Pineapple, drained, unsweetened tidbits
2 tbsp. Mustard; Dijon-style
1 tbsp. Soy sauce
1 Garlic clove, minced

Method

Arrange chicken in the crockpot. Sprinkle with pepper and paprika. Mix soy sauce, pineapple and mustard together; pour over chicken. Add minced garlic. Cover and cook on LOW for 7 to 9 hours or on HIGH for 3 to 4 hours. Serve hot. Enjoy!

Pioneer Beans

Ingredients

1 pound ground beef
1/4 pound sliced bacon, chopped
1 medium onion, chopped
1 (15-ounce) can red kidney beans, rinsed and drained
1 (15-ounce) can butter beans,, rinsed and drained

1 (15-ounce) can pork and beans in tomato sauce
1 cup ketchup
1/2 cup packed brown sugar,
1/4 cup molasses
1 tbsp. vinegar
1 tbsp. prepared mustard

Method

Place all the ingredients in the crock pot and mix well. Cover and cook on low heat setting for 5 to 6 hours, or on high heat setting for 2 hours. Serve hot. Enjoy!

Polynesian Steak Strips

Ingredients

2 lbs. beef steak, cut across the grain into thin slices
2 tbsp. Ketchup
1 tbsp. oyster sauce
1/4 cup soy sauce
1/2 tsp. ground ginger
1/4 tsp. garlic powder
1 tsp. granulated sugar
1/4 tsp. liquid gravy browner
1 tsp. Salt
1/4 tsp. Pepper

Method

Place steak strips in 3 1/2 qt. slow cooker. Mix remaining 10 ingredients in small bowl. Pour over strips and stir well. Cover and cook on LOW for 8-10 hours or on HIGH for 4 to 5 hours. Serve hot. Enjoy!

Porcupine Meatballs in Tomato Sauce

Makes 24-26 meatballs

Ingredients

2 (8 oz.) cans tomato sauce
1/4 tsp. garlic powder
1/2 tsp. ground thyme
1/2 cup water
1 1/4 lb. lean ground beef
1/2 cup long-grain rice
2 tbsp. minced onion
1/2 tsp. salt
1/4 tsp. ground black pepper

Method

Combine the tomato sauce, garlic powder, thyme and water in a 1 1/2 qt. slow cooker. In a medium bowl, combine the beef, rice, onion, salt and pepper and mix well. Shape into 24-26 balls about the size of golf balls. Place meatballs in tomato mixture in slow cooker. Cover and cook on LOW for 7-8 hours or until rice is tender. Serve by pouring sauce over meatballs. Enjoy!

Pork-and-Black Bean Chili

Ingredients

1 lb. lean boned pork loin roast
1 (16-oz) jar thick-and-chunky salsa
2 (15-oz) cans no-salt-added black beans, undrained
1 cup chopped yellow bell pepper
3/4 cup chopped onion
1 tsp. ground cumin
1 tsp. chili powder
1 tsp. dried oregano
1/4 cup fat-free sour cream

Method

Trim fat from pork; cut into 1-inch pieces. Combine pork and the next 7 ingredients in a 4-quart electric slow cooker; stir well. Cover with lid; cook on low-heat setting for 8 hours or until pork is tender. Ladle chili into bowls; top with sour cream. Serve immediately. Enjoy!

Pork Chop Dinner

Ingredients

6 pork loin chops (3/4" thick)
1 tbsp. vegetable oil
1 large onion, sliced
1 medium green pepper, chopped
1 can (4 oz.) mushrooms, drained
1 can (8 oz.) tomato sauce

1 tbsp. brown sugar
2 tsp. Worcestershire sauce
1 1/2 tsp. cider vinegar
1/2 tsp. salt
Hot cooked rice (optional)

Method

In a skillet, brown pork chops on both sides in oil; drain. Place chops in a slow cooker. Add the onion, green pepper and mushrooms. In a bowl, combine the tomato sauce, brown sugar, Worcestershire sauce, vinegar and salt. Pour over meat and vegetables. Cover and cook on low 4-5 hours or until meat is tender. Serve with rice if desired. Enjoy!

Pork Chops with Jalapeno-Pecan Cornbread Stuffing

Ingredients

6 boneless pork loin chops, 1" thick (1 1/2 lbs.)
3/4 cup chopped onion
3/4 cup chopped celery
1/2 cup coarsely chopped pecans
1/2 medium jalapeno pepper, seeded and chopped
1 tsp. rubbed sage
1/2 tsp. dried rosemary leaves
1/8 tsp. black pepper
4 cups unseasoned cornbread stuffing mix
1 1/4 cups reduced-sodium chicken broth
1 egg, lightly beaten

Method

Trim the excess fat from pork and discard. Spray large skillet with nonstick cooking spray; heat over medium heat. Add pork; cook onion, celery, pecans, jalapeno pepper, sage, rosemary and black pepper to the skillet and cook for 5 minutes or until tender. Set aside. Combine cornbread stuffing mix, vegetable mixture and broth in medium bowl. Stir in the egg. Spoon stuffing mixture into the slow cooker and arrange pork on top. Cover and cook on LOW about 5 hours or until pork is tender and barley pink in the center. Serve hot. Enjoy!

Pork Chops and Potatoes in Mustard Sauce

Ingredients

6 4-ounce pork loin chops, trimmed
1 (10 3/4-ounce) can Campbell's 98% Fat Free Cream of Mushroom Soup
1/4 cup low sodium chicken broth
1/4 cup Dijon mustard
1/2 tsp. dried thyme
1 clove garlic,, minced, or 1/4 tsp. garlic powder
1/4 tsp. black pepper
6 medium potatoes,, thinly sliced
1 onion, sliced

Method

In skillet, brown pork chops in 2 tbsp. oil. Drain the fat. Place the soup, chicken broth, mustard, thyme, garlic, and pepper in a crockpot. Add the potatoes and onion, stirring to coat. Place the browned pork chops on top of potato mixture. Cover and cook on LOW for 8 to 10 hours or on HIGH 4 to 5 hours. Serve hot. Enjoy!

Pot of Pizza

Ingredients

8 ounces extra lean ground beef or turkey
1/2 cup chopped onion
1/2 cup chopped green pepper
1/2 cup (one 2.5 ounce jar) sliced mushrooms, drained
1 3/4 cup (one 15-ounce can) Hunt's Tomato Sauce <-- I used Hunt's pizza sauce
1 tsp. Italian Seasoning
1 tsp. pourable Spenda
3 cups cooked noodles, rinsed and drained
1/4 cup shredded Kraft reduced-fat Cheddar cheese
1/4 cup shredded Kraft reduced-fat Mozzarella cheese

Method

In a large skillet, sprayed with olive-oil-flavored cooking spray, brown the meat, onion and green pepper together. Stir in the mushrooms, tomato sauce, Italian seasoning and Splenda. Pour mixture into a slow cooker sprayed with butter-flavored cooking spray. Spread the noodles over meat mixture and sprinkle with Parmesan cheese. Layer cheddar and mozzarella cheeses evenly over the top. Cover and cook on LOW for 6-8 hours. Mix well before serving. Enjoy!

Pot Roast

Ingredients

4 large potatoes, , cut into chunks
4 large carrots,, cut into chunks
2 large onions,, cut into chunks
2 cups rutabaga,, cut into chunks
3 pounds boneless beef chuck roast (or other),, trimmed
1/2 cup boiling water
1 tsp. beef bouillon granules
1/2 tsp. Liquid gravy browner

Method

Place the potatoes, carrots, rutabaga and onions in bottom of 5 quart slow cooker. Place roast on top. Combine remaining 3 ingredients in small bowl. Mix well and pour over the meat and vegetables. Cover and cook on LOW for 10 to 12 hours or on HIGH for 5 to 6 hours. Enjoy!

Potato & Leek Chowder

Ingredients

3 medium potatoes,, peeled and diced
11 ounces canned corn, drained
1/2 cup chopped celery
1 packet leek soup
4 cups water
1 cup nonfat dry milk powder
1/2 cup shredded Swiss cheese

Method

In slow cooker, combine the potatoes, corn, celery, dry leek soup mix and water and mix well. Cover and cook on LOW for 5 to 6 hours or until potatoes and celery are tender. Just before serving, gradually add dry milk powder to the hot soup and gently whisk until well blended. Ladle into individual soup bowls; sprinkle with cheese, if desired. Enjoy!

Potato and Mushroom Chowder

Ingredients

1/2 cup onion,, chopped
1/4 cup reduced-calorie margarine
2 tbsp. flour
1 tsp. salt
1/2 tsp. black pepper
2 cups water

8 ounces sliced mushrooms, drained,
1 cup celery, chopped
2 cups potatoes,, peeled and diced
1 cup carrots,, chopped
2 cups skim milk
1/4 cup fat-free Parmesan cheese,, grated

Method

In a skillet, sauté the onion and celery in the margarine until the onion is translucent. Remove from heat. Add the flour, salt and pepper and stir well. Place in crock pot and add in the water, potatoes, mushrooms, and carrots. Cover and cook on low for 6-8 hours (or on high for 3-4 hours). If on low, turn to high after cooking time is over. Add the milk and Parmesan cheese and cook another 30 minutes. Serve hot. Enjoy!

Red Beans and Rice

Ingredients

1 lb. dried kidney beans (2 cups), sorted and rinsed
1 large green bell pepper, chopped
1 large onion, chopped
2 cloves garlic, finely chopped

7 cups water
1 1/2 tsp. Salt
1/4 tsp. Pepper
2 cups uncooked instant rice
Red pepper sauce

Method

Mix all ingredients except rice and pepper sauce in 3 1/2-6 qt. slow cooker. Cover and cook on HIGH for 4-5 hours or until beans are tender. Stir in the rice. Cover and cook on HIGH for 15 to 20 min. or until rice is tender. Serve with pepper sauce. Enjoy!

Refried Beans

Ingredients

2 lb. dried pinto beans

2-3 onions, quartered
1 tbsp. salt water
3-4 slices bacon, cut into chunks (optional)
2 chopped peppers (optional)

Method

Pour the beans in a large pot and add water to cover the beans. Allow the beans to soak for at least eight hours. Add all ingredients except salt to the crockpot. Cover and cook on high for 3-4 hours or until beans are very soft and tender. Add salt at around the 2.5 hour mark. Serve hot. Enjoy!

Rustic Vegetable Soup

Ingredients

16 ounces picante sauce,
10 ounces frozen mixed vegetables, 10 ounces frozen green beans, cut and thawed
10 ounces fat-free beef broth
2 medium baking potatoes, , cut into 1/2" pieces
1 medium green bell pepper,, chopped
1/2 tsp. sugar
1/4 cup parsley

Method

Combine all ingredients, except parsley, in slow cooker. Cover and cook on LOW for 8 hours or on HIGH for 4 hours. Stir in the parsley; serve immediately. Enjoy!

Salsa Chicken

Ingredients

1 lb. boneless, skinless chicken breasts
1 jar salsa
2 tbsp. Flour

Method

Layer chicken and salsa in crockpot ending with salsa. Cook on low 10-12 hours. When ready to serve, turn crockpot to high and stir in 2tbsp. of flour. Cook until thickened. I serve this with rice (4 pints per cup). If you have leftovers, shred chicken and put it in a low fat flour tortilla with fat free sour cream and fat free shredded cheese. Enjoy!

Sausage Pasta Stew

Ingredients

1 lb. turkey Italian Sausage links, casing removed
4 cups water
1 jar (26 oz.) meatless spaghetti sauce
1 can (16 oz.) kidney beans, rinsed and drained
1 medium yellow summer squash, halved lengthwise and cut into 1-inch pieces
2 medium carrots, cut into 1/4 inch slices
1 medium sweet red or green pepper, diced
1/3 cup chopped onion
1 1/2 cups uncooked spiral pasta
1 cup frozen peas
1 tsp. sugar
1/2 tsp. salt
1/4 tsp. pepper

Method

In a nonstick skillet, cook the sausage over medium heat until no longer pink; drain and place in a 5qt slow cooker. Add water, spaghetti sauce, beans, summer squash, carrots, red pepper and onion; mix well. Cover and cook on low for 7-9 hours or until vegetables are tender. Stir in the pasta, peas, sugar, salt and pepper; mix well. Cover and cook on high for 15-20 minutes or until pasta is tender. Serve hot.0 Enjoy!

Sausage and Sauerkraut Dinner

Ingredients

6 small red potatoes, unpeeled, quartered
8 fresh baby carrots, cut into 1/4" slices
1 medium onion, cut into thin wedges
1 tbsp. brown sugar
1 tbsp. spicy brown mustard
1 tsp. caraway seeds
1 (15 oz.) can sauerkraut
1 lb. fully cooked turkey kielbasa, cut into 1" slices

Method

In a 3 1/2-4 quarts slow cooker, combine the potatoes, carrots, and onion. In a medium bowl, combine brown sugar, mustard, and caraway seed, mix well. Stir in sauerkraut and kielbasa. Spoon this mixture over vegetables in cooker. Cover, cook on LOW for at least 8 hours. Serve hot. Enjoy!

Savory Beef Fajitas

Ingredients

1 beef flank steak (2 lbs.) thinly sliced
1 cup tomato juice
2 garlic cloves, minced
1 tbsp. minced fresh cilantro or parsley
1 tsp. chili powder
1 tsp. ground cumin
1/2 tsp. salt

1/2 tsp. ground coriander
1 medium onion, sliced
1 medium green pepper, julienne
1 medium jalapeno, cut into thin strips
12 flour tortillas (7")
Sour cream, guacamole, salsa or shredded Cheddar cheese, optional

Method

Place the beef in a slow cooker. Combine the next 7 ingredients in a bowl and pour over beef. Cover and cook on LOW for 6-7 hours. Add the onions, pepper and jalapeno and cover and cook for 1 hour longer or until meat and vegetables are tender. Using a slotted spoon, place about 1/2 cup of the meat vegetable mixture on each tortilla. Add desired toppings. Roll up. Enjoy!

Savory Pot Roast

Ingredients

3-3 1/2 pound beef boneless chuck roast
1 tbsp. vegetable oil
8 small red potatoes, cut in half
3 cups baby-cut carrots
1 large onion, coarsely chopped
1 jar (5 ounces) prepared horseradish
1 tsp. salt
1/2 tsp. pepper
1 cup water

Method

Trim the fat from the roast and discard. Heat oil in skillet over medium-high heat and cook the beef in the oil for about 10 minutes, turning occasionally, until brown on all sides. Place the potatoes, carrots and onion in 4-6 quart slow cooker. Place beef on the bed of vegetables. Mix in the horseradish, salt and pepper; spread evenly over beef. Pour water over the beef and vegetables. Cover and cook on low heat setting for 8-10 hours or until beef and vegetables are tender. Serve hot. Enjoy!

Sirloin Tip Casserole

Ingredients

2 1/2 lbs. sirloin tips
1 can Campbell's golden mushroom soup mix
1 package Onion Soup Mix
Small whole potatoes, as per your taste

Method

In a crock pot mix together the sirloin tips, golden mushroom soup mix, and the onion soup mix. Peel as many small whole potatoes as you desire and place on top of meat mixture, turning them once to cover with the soup mixture so they will brown nicely. Cook on low for 8-10 hours or until the meat is tender. Serve with your favorite vegetable and crusty bread. Enjoy!

Slow Cooked Beef Burgundy

Ingredients

1/3 cup All Purpose Flour
1 tsp. salt
1/4 tsp. pepper
2 lb. cubed beef stew meat
1 1/2 cups fresh baby carrots, halved crosswise
1 (10-oz.) package fresh pearl onions, peeled

1 (8-oz.) package small fresh whole mushrooms
1 garlic clove, minced
1 bay leaf
1 (10 1/2-oz.) can condensed beef consommé
1 1/2 cup water
Fresh oregano, if desired

Method

In a 3 1/2 or 4-quart slow cooker, combine the flour, salt, pepper and beef; mix well. Add all remaining ingredients and stir well. Cover and cook on LOW setting for 10 to 12 hours or until carrots and beef are tender. Garnish with oregano. Enjoy!

Slow Cooked Chicken and Sausage Stew

Ingredients

½ lb. Kielbasa sausage, cut into ¼ inch slices
2 boneless, skinless chicken breast halves, cut into bite size strips
½ cup thinly sliced carrot
1 small onion, thinly sliced, separated into rings
1 (16 oz.) can baked beans, undrained
2 tbsp. brown sugar
1 tsp. dry mustard
½ cup ketchup
1 tbsp. vinegar
2 cups frozen cut green beans, thawed

Method

In a 3 ½ to 4 quart Crock Pot, combine all the ingredients except green beans. Cover and cook on low setting for 6 to 8 hours or until chicken is no longer pink. Ten minutes before serving, stir in green beans. Increase to high heat setting; cover and cook an additional 10 minutes or until green beans are crisp tender. Serve hot. Enjoy!

Slow Cooked Chicken Cacciatore

Ingredients

4 chicken thighs, skin removed if desired
4 chicken legs, skin removed if desired
1 (15-oz.) can chunky Italian-style tomato sauce
1 (4.5 Oz) jar green giant whole mushrooms, drained
1 tsp. dried oregano leaves
1 small onion, sliced
1 small green bell pepper, cut into 1-inch pieces
2 garlic cloves, minced
1/4 cup water
2 tbsp. Pillsbury Best' All Purpose or Unbleached Flour

Method

In a 4 quart slow cooker combine all ingredients except, water and flour, and mix gently. Cover and cook on low setting for 6 to 8 hours. With a slotted spoon, remove chicken and vegetables from slow cooker and place in serving bowl. Cover to keep warm. In a small bowl, combine the water and flour and blend well. Stir into the liquid in the slow cooker. Increase the heat to high; cover and cook for an additional 5 to 10 min. or till thickened. Stir well; spoon mixture over chicken. If desired, serve with hot cooked pasta. Enjoy!

Slow Cooked Garlic Chicken

Ingredients

4 skinned chicken breast halves
1 tsp. salt
2 tsp. paprika
2 tsp. lemon pepper
1 large onion, sliced
10 cloves garlic, un-peeled

Method

Mix together the salt, pepper and paprika. Rub the mix all over the chicken breast. Place the onion in a slow cooker. Place chicken breast side up on the onion. Place the garlic on chicken and cover and cook on low in the slow cooker for about 6 hours or until juices run clear. Serve hot. Enjoy!

Slow Cooked Honey-Dijon Pork Roast

Ingredients

1/2 cup chopped onion
2 apples, peeled and sliced
1 tbsp. Honey
1 tbsp. Dijon mustard
1/2 tsp. coriander seed, crushed
1/4 tsp. Salt
1 (2 to 2 1/2 lb.) rolled boneless pork roast
1 tbsp. Cornstarch
2 tbsp. Water

Method

In 4 to 6 qt. slow cooker, combine the onion and apples. In small bowl, combine the honey, mustard, coriander and salt; mix well. Spread on all sides of pork roast; place roast over onions and apples. Cover and cook on LOW for 7-8 hours. Remove thee roast from the slow cooker and place on serving platter. Cover with a foil. In small saucepan, combine cornstarch and water, blend well. Add apple mixture and juices from slow cooker; mix well. Cook and heat over medium heat until the mixture boils, stirring occasionally. Cut roast into slices. Serve with sauce. Enjoy!

Slow Cooked Sweet & Sour Pork

Ingredients

1 1/2 pounds pork loins, lean, boneless and cut into cubes
8 ounces canned pineapple chunks in juice, undralned (unsweetened juice)
1 medium red bell pepper, cut into squares
3 tbsp. brown sugar
1/2 tsp. ginger
1/4 cup vinegar
3 tbsp. soy sauce
3 tbsp. water
2 tbsp. cornstarch
2 cups cooked rice

Method

In a 3-1/2 to 4 quart slow cooker, combine the pork, pineapple, bell pepper, brown sugar, ginger, vinegar and soy sauce and mix well. Cover and cook on LOW setting for 6 to 8 hours. About 5 minutes before serving, in a small bowl, combine 3 tbsp. water and cornstarch and blend well. Stir into pork mixture in slow cooker. Cover and cook on high setting for an additional 5 minutes or until thickened. Serve pork mixture over rice. Makes 4 servings. Prepare rice 25 minutes before serving. Serve hot. Enjoy!

Dinner Recipes

Slow-Cooked Turkey Dinner

Ingredients

6 small red potatoes, unpeeled, quartered (about 2 1/2 inches in diameter)
2 cups sliced carrots
1 1/2 pounds turkey dark meat, skinless, (turkey thighs)
1/4 cup all-purpose flour
2 tbsp. dry onion soup mix
1/3 cup chicken broth
1 can condensed reduced fat cream of mushroom soup

Method

Place the potatoes and carrots in a 3-1/2 or 4 quart Crock-Pot Slow Cooker. Place the turkey thighs over vegetables. In medium bowl, combine flour and remaining ingredients; blend well. Pour this mix over the turkey. Cover and cook on high setting for 30 minutes. Reduce setting to low and cook for at least 7 hours or until turkey is fork tender. With slotted spoon, remove turkey and vegetables from slow cooker and place on a serving platter. Stir sauce until smooth and pour over turkey and vegetables.

NOTES: For best results: Fill your slow cooker only half to three-quarters full.

Use lean meats, trimming any extra fat, and skinless poultry to reduce the fat in slow-cooked meals.

Thaw frozen ingredients in your microwave before adding them to the slow cooker, so they'll cook thoroughly.

Remove the lid only to stir food. Lifting the lid releases heat, and the dish may require additional cooking time. Enjoy!

Autumn Vegetable Minestrone

Ingredients

2 (14.5 oz.) cans vegetable broth
1 (18 oz.) can crushed tomatoes, undrained
3 medium carrots, chopped
3 small zucchini, cut into 1/2" slices
1 medium yellow bell pepper, cut into 1/2" pieces
8 medium green onions, sliced
2 cloves garlic, finely chopped
2 cups shredded cabbage
2 tsp. dried marjoram
1 tsp. salt

1/4 tsp. pepper
1 cup uncooked instant rice
1/4 cup chopped fresh basil

Method

Mix all the ingredients except rice and basil in a 3 ½ to 6 quart slow cooker. Cover and cook on low heat setting for 6 to 8 hours or until vegetables are tender. Stir in the rice. Cover and cook on low heat setting for about 15 minutes or until rice is tender. Enjoy!

Beef And Broccoli

Ingredients

1 pound boneless beef top round steak, trimmed of fat, cut into cubes
1 (4.5-ounce) jar sliced mushrooms, drained
1 medium onion, cut into wedges
1/2 cup condensed beef broth
3 tbsp. teriyaki baste and glaze
1 tbsp. sesame seed
1 tsp. dark sesame oil, if desired
2/3 cup uncooked regular long-grain white rice
1 1/3 cups water
2 tbsp. water
1 tbsp. cornstarch
2 cups green frozen 100% broccoli florets

Method

In a 3 1/2 to 4-quart slow cooker, combine beef, mushrooms, onion, broth, teriyaki baste and glaze, sesame seed and sesame oil and mix well. Cover and cook on low setting for 8 to 10 hours. About 35 minutes before serving, cook rice in 1 1/3 cups water as directed on package. Meanwhile, in small bowl, combine 2 tbsp. water and cornstarch; blend well. Stir the cornstarch mixture and broccoli into beef mixture. Cover; cook on low setting for an additional 30 minutes or until broccoli is crisp-tender. Serve over rice. Enjoy!

Beef and Pasta

Ingredients

2 (14 oz.) cans tomatoes with juice, broken up

1 1/2 cups water
1 tsp. parsley flakes
1/4 tsp. garlic powder
1/4 tsp. onion powder
1 tsp. Salt
1/ tsp. Pepper
1 tsp. liquid gravy browner
1 1/2 lbs. lean ground beef
8 oz. Rotini pasta

Method

Combine first 8 ingredients in a large bowl and stir well. Add the ground beef and mix. Pour into a 3 1/2 quart slow cooker. Cover and cook on LOW for 6 to 8 hours or HIGH for 3 to 4 hours. Add pasta and stir. Cook on HIGH for 15 to 20 minutes until tender. Enjoy!

Beef Tips in Mushroom Sauce

Ingredients

2 pounds lean chuck, cut in 1, 3/4 inch pieces
1 can 98% fat free cream of mushroom soup
1 package onion soup mix
1 can sugar free sprite or 7up

Method

Put the meat in crock pot. Pour in the soup and onion soup mix over meat. Add in the Sugar Free Sprite/7up. Cook in crock pot all day on low (or high for at least 4 hours). Turn off and let sit for 30 minutes before serving. I added canned sliced mushrooms (drained) and served over rice. Enjoy!

Cabbage Roll Soup

Ingredients

1 pound ground round
3 1/2 cups water
2 cups coarsely chopped green cabbage
1 cup sliced carrot
1/2 cup sliced celery
1/2 cup chopped onion

1/2 tsp. dried dill
1/2 tsp. dried oregano
1/2 tsp. dried basil
1/2 tsp. pepper
3 cans beef consommé- undiluted--10.5 ounces per can
2 cans diced tomatoes -undrained--14.5 ounces per can
1/2 cup uncooked converted rice

Method

Brown meat in a nonstick skillet over medium-high heat and drain well. Place the meat in a 4-quart electric slow cooker; stir in water and next 10 ingredients. Cover and cook on low-heat for 8 hours. Increase heat setting to high and stir in the rice. Cover and cook for an additional 30 minutes or until rice is tender. Enjoy!

California Vegetable Cheese Bake

Ingredients

4 cups frozen carrot, broccoli & cauliflower blend, thawed
1/2 cup finely chopped onion (can use frozen chopped onion)
1 (10-3/4 oz.) can cream of mushroom soup
1/4 cup (one 2-ounce jar) chopped pimiento, drained
1-1/2 cups cubed processed cheese

Method

Spray a slow cooker container with butter-flavored cooking spray. In the prepared container, combine the thawed vegetables & onion. Add the mushroom soup, pimiento & cheese. Mix well to combine. Cover & cook on LOW for 4 to 6 hours. Mix well before serving. Enjoy!

Chicken & Macaroni w/mushrooms

Ingredients

1 (10 3/4 oz.) can cream of chicken soup
1/4 cup no-fat sour cream
16 oz. skinned & boned uncooked chicken breast, cut into 20 pieces
1 cup (one 4oz. can) sliced mushrooms, drained
1/2 cup finely chopped onion
1 1/3 cups (3oz) uncooked elbow macaroni

Method

Spray a slow cooker container with butter flavored cooking spray. In the prepared container, combine chicken soup & sour cream. Add in rest of the ingredients and mix well. Cover & cook on LOW for 6 to 8 hours. Gently stir again just before serving. Enjoy!

Chicken Noodle Soup

Ingredients

3/4 pound boneless, skinless chicken thighs, cut into 1" pieces
2 cups sliced celery
2 cups chopped carrots
3/4 cup chopped onion
14 1/2 ounces ready-to-serve chicken broth

1/2 tsp. dried marjoram, crushed
1 tsp. dried thyme leaves, crushed
1/2 tsp. salt, optional
2 bay leaves
10 ounces frozen green peas
1 cup frozen home-style egg noodles

Method

Spray 10-inch skillet with cooking spray and heat over medium heat. Cook the chicken in skillet 5 minutes, stirring frequently, until brown. Mix the chicken and remaining ingredients, except peas and noodles, in a 3-1/2 to 4 quart slow cooker. Cover and cook on low heat setting for 6 1/2 to 7 hours or until chicken is no longer pink in center. Stir in peas and noodles and cook for about 10 minutes longer or until noodles are tender. I love using the old fashioned flavor of the home-style noodles, but if they aren't available use 1 cup of uncooked fine egg noodles or instant rice. Enjoy!

Chicken Noodle Soup #2

Ingredients

1 chicken whole, no skin, cut up
2 medium Carrots, peeled and chopped
1/2 cup onion, peeled and chopped
2 Stalks celery, coarsely chopped
2 1/2 tsp. Salt
2 tsp. parsley
3/4 tsp. marjoram
1/2 tsp. basil
1/4 tsp. Poultry seasoning
1/4 tsp. Pepper

1 Bay leaf
2 quarts water
2 1/2 cup egg noodles

Method

Place the first 4 ingredients in a 3 1/2-quart slow cooker in the order listed. Combine salt and the next 6 ingredients and sprinkle over vegetables. Add 6 cups water; cover and cook on low setting for 8 to 10 hours. Remove the chicken and bay leaf; add remaining 2 cups of water. Stir in the noodles and cook, covered, on high setting for 20 minutes. Meanwhile remove bones from the chicken and cut chicken into bite-size pieces. Add to slow cooker, stir to mix. Cook for 15 minutes on high setting, covered or until noodles are tender. Enjoy!

Chicken Veggie Soup

Ingredients

1 1/2 boned and skinless chicken breast
3 carrots, diced
3 potatoes, diced
1 onion, chopped
2 cups anise root, chopped
2 cups cabbage, chopped
10 ounces low fat chicken broth (1 can Campbell's)

Water, just enough to cover
2 bay leaves
Salt and pepper, to taste
Garlic, to taste
Italian seasoning, to taste
3 chili peppers, dried

Method

Place all the ingredients in a slow cooker and cook on low for about 8-10 hours or until the veggies are cooked. Remove the red peppers and serve immediately. Enjoy!

Chicken-Vegetable Chowder

Ingredients

1 pound boneless skinless chicken thighs, cut in 1" pieces
1 cup fresh baby carrots, cut in halves, lengthwise
1 cup sliced fresh mushrooms
1/2 cup chopped onion
1/2 cup water
1/4 tsp. garlic powder
1/8 tsp. dried thyme leaves
1 14 1/2oz can ready-to-serve chicken broth
1 10 3/4oz.can condensed cream of chicken & broccoli soup 98% Fat Free, with 30% less sodium
1/2 cup milk

3 tbsp. all-purpose flour
1 9 oz. package Green Giant Harvest Fresh Cut Broccoli, thawed

Method

In a 3 1/2 to 4 quart crock pot slow cooker, combine the chicken, carrots, mushrooms, onion, water, garlic powder, thyme and broth and mix well. Cover and cook on low setting for 7 to 9 hours or until chicken is no longer pink. Drain the fat from slow cooker. In a small bowl, combine the soup, milk and flour and beat with a wire whisk until smooth. Add the soup mixture and broccoli to the chicken mixture. Cover and cook for an additional 30 minutes or until broccoli is tender. Enjoy!

Chinese Beef And Pea Pods

Ingredients

1 pound flank steak
10 1/2 ounces beef consommé
1/4 cup soy sauce
1/4 tsp. ground ginger
1 bunch green onions, sliced
2 tbsp. cornstarch
2 tbsp. cold water
7 ounces Snow Peas, frozen, partially thawed

Method

Thinly slice the flank steak diagonally across the grain. Combine the strips in a slow cooking pot with the consommé, soy sauce, ginger and onions. Cover and cook on low for 5 to 7 hours. Turn the slow cooker controls to high. Stir in cornstarch that has been dissolved in the cold water. Cook on high for 10 to 15 minutes or until thickened. Drop in the pea pods in the last 5 minutes. Serve over hot rice. Enjoy!

Chinese Beef and Vegetable Stew

Ingredients

4 cups shredded cabbage, packed
1 large green bell pepper, cut into thin strips
1 (4 1/2 ounces) jar canned mushrooms
6 scallions, chopped

1 can, (8 ounces) water chestnut, canned and drained
1 pound lean round steak, cut into strips
1/4 cup dry sherry
3 tbsp. soy sauce
3 tbsp. water

3 tbsp. hoisin sauce
1 tsp. Chinese chili paste with garlic
1/4 tsp. garlic powder
1/4 tsp. garlic pepper

1 1/2 tbsp. cornstarch
16 ounces frozen young green beans, thawed
1/2 large red bell pepper, chopped

Method

In a 31/2- or 4-quart electric slow cooker, mix together the cabbage, green pepper, mushrooms, scallions, water chestnuts, and beef. In a small bowl, mix together 2 tbsp. each of the sherry and soy sauce, water, hoisin sauce, chili paste and garlic powder. Pour over the beef and vegetables in the pot. Sprinkle with the garlic pepper. Cover and cook on the low heat setting for 5 1/2 to 6 hours. In a small bowl or cup, mix together the cornstarch and remaining sherry and soy sauce. Increase the heat setting to high. Stir in the cornstarch mixture. Place cover slightly ajar and cook on high for 1/2 hour, stirring once or twice, until the sauce clears and thickens slightly. Stir in the green beans and red pepper and cook for 5 to 10 minutes longer. Serve over hot steamed rice. Enjoy!

Chops in a Crock Pot

Ingredients

6 whole pork loin chops, browned
1 whole onion, chopped
3 tbsp. ketchup

10 1/2 oz. 98% fat-free cream of chicken soup
2 tbsp. Worcestershire sauce

Method

Place all the ingredients into crock pot and cook on LOW about 4-5 hours. Serve with rice, noodles or potatoes. Enjoy!

Slow Cooker Hot German Potato Salad

Ingredients

5 medium potatoes (about 1 3/4 lbs.), cut into 1/4" slices
1 large onion, chopped
1/3 cup water
1/3 cup cider vinegar
2 tbsp. all-purpose flour
2 tbsp. Sugar
1 tsp. Salt
1/2 tsp. celery seed

1/4 tsp. Pepper

4 slices crisply cooked bacon, crumbled

Method

Mix the potatoes and onion in a 3 1/2-6 quart slow cooker. Mix in the remaining ingredients except bacon and pour into cooker. Cover and cook on LOW 8-10 hours or until the potatoes are tender. Stir in the bacon. Serve hot. Enjoy!

Slow Cooker-Marinara Sauce with Spaghetti

Ingredients

2 cans (28 oz. each) crushed tomatoes with Italian herbs

1 can (6 oz.) tomato paste

1 large onion, chopped (1 cup)

8 cloves garlic, finely chopped

1 tbsp. olive oil or vegetable oil

2 tsp. Sugar

1 tsp. dried oregano leaves

1 tsp. Salt

1 tsp. Pepper

12 cups hot cooked spaghetti, for serving

Shredded Parmesan cheese, if desired

Method

Mix all ingredients except spaghetti and cheese in a 3 1/2 to 6 quarts slow cooker. Cover and cook on LOW 8 to 10 hours (or HIGH 4 to 5 hours). Serve over spaghetti. Sprinkle with cheese. Enjoy!

Slow Cooker Meat Loaf

Ingredients

24 ounces extra lean ground turkey or beef

1 cup finely chopped onion

4 slices reduced-calorie white bread, torn into small pieces

2 tsp. prepared yellow mustard

1 tbsp. pourable Splenda or Sugar Twin

1 tsp. dried parsley flakes

1 cup (one 8-ounce can) Hunt's Tomato Sauce

Method

Spray a slow cooker container with butter-flavored cooking spray. In a large bowl, combine the meat, onion, bread pieces, mustard, and 1/2 cup tomato sauce. Mix well to combine. Form into a large ball. Place in the prepared slow cooker container. Stir Splenda and parsley flakes into the remaining 1/2 cup tomato sauce and spoon mixture evenly over meat loaf. Cover and cook on LOW for 6 to 8 hours. Divide into 8 servings. When serving, evenly spoon sauce over top. Enjoy!

Slow Cooker Paprika Chicken in Wine

Ingredients

1/2 cup dry white wine
2 tsp. olive oil
1 lb. Boneless, skinless chicken breasts, trimmed of fat and cut into 4 pcs.
1 tsp. cumin seeds
1 tsp. mustard seeds
4 cloves garlic, minced
1 tbsp. Paprika
1 large onion, thinly sliced
4 oz. mushrooms, sliced
Sprigs of parsley for garnish
Sweet red pepper rings, for garnish

Method

Pour the wine into the crockery pot. Heat 1 tbsp. of the oil in a skillet, and brown the chicken on both sides over medium-high heat for 3-5 minutes. Transfer the chicken to the crock pot, and sprinkle on the cumin, mustard, garlic and paprika. Add the remaining oil to the same skillet and sauté the onions and mushrooms until lightly browned, 2-3 minutes. Spoon this mixture over the chicken. Cover and cook on LOW until the chicken is tender, 7-9 hours. Garnish with the parsley and peppers. Enjoy!

Slow Cooker Pierogies in Pepper-Shallot Sauce

Ingredients

1 can (28 oz.) crushed tomatoes
1 shallot, thinly sliced
1 cup chopped sweet green peppers
1/2 tsp. olive oil
1/2 tbsp. red wine vinegar

1/2 tsp. Italian herb seasoning
1/2 tsp. black pepper
1 lb. potato-filled pierogies, fresh or frozen (thawed)

Method

Combine the first 7 ingredients in the crock pot. Cover and cook on LOW for 5-9 hours or on HIGH for 3 1/2 to 5 hours. Add the pierogies. Cover and cook for 1 hr. Serve hot. Enjoy!

Slow Cooker Pork Roast with Creamy Mustard Sauce

Ingredients

2 1/2-3 lb. pork boneless sirloin roast
1 tbsp. vegetable oil
3/4 cup dry white wine
2 tbsp. all-purpose flour
1 tsp. Salt
1/2 tsp. Pepper
2 medium carrots, finely chopped or shredded
1 medium onion, finely chopped (1/2 cup)
1 small shallot, finely chopped (2 tbsp.)
1/4 cup half-and-half
2 to 3 tbsp. country-style Dijon mustard

Method

Trim excess fat from pork. Heat oil in a 10" skillet over med.-high heat and cook pork in the oil for about 10 minutes, turning occasionally, until brown on all sides. Place the pork in a 3 1/2-6 quart slow cooker. Mix in the remaining ingredients except the half-and-half and mustard; pour over pork. Cover and cook on LOW 7-9 hours or until pork is tender. Remove the pork from the cooker; cover and keep warm. Skim fat from pork juices in cooker, if desired. Stir half-and-half and mustard into juices. Cover and cook on HIGH about 15 minutes or until slightly thickened. Serve sauce with pork. Enjoy!

Slow Cooker Salmon Patties

Ingredients

2 large eggs, fork beaten
2.75 oz. can salmon, drained, skin and round bones removed
1/2 cup water

1 cup soda cracker crumbs
1/2 tsp. celery salt
1/2 tsp. onion powder
1/4 tsp. Salt
1/4 tsp. dill weed
1/16 tsp. Pepper
1/2 cup cornflake crumbs

Method

Combine the first 9 ingredients in a bowl and shape into 8 patties. Coat the patties with cornflake crumbs. Place 4 patties on bottom of a 3 1/2 or 5 qt. slow cooker and place remaining patties on top. Cover and cook on low for 4-5 hours or on HIGH for 2 to 2 -1/2 hrs. Serve hot. Enjoy!

Slow Cooker Salsa Swiss Steak

Ingredients

2 tsp. oil
1 1/2 lbs. boneless beef top round steak, trimmed of fat, cut into 5 pcs.
1/2 tsp. Salt
1/4 tsp. Pepper
1 medium onion, halved lengthwise, sliced

1/2 medium green bell pepper, cut into bite-size strips
1 (10 3/4 oz.) can condensed cream of mushroom soup
3/4 cup thick and chunky salsa

Method

Heat oil in large skillet over medium-high heat until the pan starts smoking. Sprinkle the steak with salt and pepper. Place the steak in skillet, cook 4-6 min. or until well browned, turning once. Transfer the steak to a 4-6 quart slow cooker. Top with onion and bell pepper. In same skillet, combine soup and salsa; mix well. Pour over vegetables and steak. Cover; cook on LOW for 8-10 hours. Remove the steak pieces from slow cooker and place on serving platter. Stir sauce well and serve with steak. Enjoy!

Slow Cooker-Sausage and Sauerkraut Dinner

Ingredients

6 small red potatoes, unpeeled, quartered
8 fresh baby carrots, cut into 1/4" slices
1 medium onion, cut into thin wedges

1 tbsp. brown sugar

1 tbsp. spicy brown mustard

1 tsp. caraway seeds

1 (15 oz.) can sauerkraut

1 lb. fully-cooked turkey kielbasa, cut into 1" slices

Method

In a 3 1/2-4 quart slow cooker, combine the potatoes, carrots and onion. In a medium bowl, combine brown sugar, mustard and caraway seed; mix well. Stir in sauerkraut and kielbasa. Spoon sauerkraut mixture over vegetables in cooker. Cover and cook on LOW for at least 8 hours or until vegetables are tender. Enjoy!

Slow Cooker Scalloped Potatoes

Ingredients

6 medium potatoes (2 lb.), cut into 1/8" slices

1 can (10 3/4 oz.) condensed cream of onion soup

1 can (5 oz.) evaporated milk (2/3 cup)

1 jar (2 oz.) diced pimientos, undrained

1/2 tsp. Salt

1/4 tsp. Pepper

Method

Spray inside of a 3 1/2-6 quart slow cooker with cooking spray. Mix all ingredients; pour into cooker. Cover and cook on LOW 10-12 hours or until potatoes are tender. Makes 8 servings Enjoy!

Slow Cooker Scalloped Potatoes and Ham

Ingredients

6 cups Frozen Shredded Potatoes (Ore Ida Hash Browns (Southern Style) Fat Free, 32 oz. bag).

1 cup Peas, frozen

1 1/2 cups Ham, extra lean, diced

1 1/2 cups Cheddar Cheese, Kraft Reduced Fat, shredded

1 can Cream of Mushroom Soup, condensed

2/3 cup Nonfat Dry Milk Powder

1 cup Water

1/4 cup Onion, diced

1 tsp. Dried Parsley

Method

In a slow cooker, combine the potatoes, peas, ham, and cheddar cheese. In a medium bowl, combine the mushroom soup, dry milk powder, water, onion, and parsley flakes. Add soup mixture to potato mixture. Mix well to combine. Cover and cook on low for 6 to 8 hours. Enjoy!

Slow Cooker Scalloped Potatoes and Turkey

Ingredients

1 lb. ground turkey breast
1/2 tsp. ground thyme
1/8 tsp. pepper
1 package (7.8 oz.) Hungry Jack Cheesy Scalloped Potatoes
2 tbsp. margarine or butter
2 1/2 cups boiling water
1 1/2 cups skim milk
1 medium red bell pepper, seeded, chopped
1 medium onion, thinly sliced

Method

Spray a large skillet with nonstick cooking spray. Heat over medium-high heat and add ground the turkey and cook until browned and no longer pink. Stir in the thyme and pepper. In large bowl, combine the sauce mix from potato package, potato slices and margarine. Add boiling water; stir until margarine melts. Add milk; mix well. Stir in browned turkey, bell pepper and onion. Spoon mixture into a 3 1/2 or 4 quart slow cooker. With back of spoon, press down potatoes to cover with sauce. Cover; cook on LOW for at least 7 hours or until potatoes are tender. Enjoy!

Slow Cooker Sloppy Joes

Ingredients

3 lbs. ground beef
1 large onion, coarsely chopped
3/4 cup chopped celery
1 cup barbecue sauce
1 can (26 1/2 oz.) sloppy Joe sauce
24 hamburger buns

Method

Cook beef and onion in Dutch oven over medium heat, stirring occasionally, until beef is brown; drain. Mix beef mixture and remaining ingredients except buns in 3 1/2-6 qt. slow cooker. Cover and cook on Low 7-9 hours (or HIGH 3 to 4 hours) or until vegetables are tender. Uncover and cook on HIGH until desired consistency. Stir well before serving. Fill buns with beef mixture. Enjoy!

Slow Cooker Steak Burritos

Ingredients

2 flank steaks (about 1 lb. each)
2 envelopes reduced-sodium taco seasoning
1 medium onion, chopped
1 can (4 oz.) chopped green chilies
1 tbsp. vinegar

10 fat-free flour tortillas (7")
1 ½ cups (6 oz.) reduced-fat shredded Monterey Jack cheese
1 1/2 cups chopped seeded plum tomatoes
3/4 cup nonfat sour cream

Method

Cut steaks in half; rub with taco seasoning. Place in slow cooker coated with nonstick cooking spray. Top with onion, chilies, and vinegar. Cover and cook on LOW for 8-9 hours or until meat is tender. Remove steaks and cool slightly; shred meat with 2 forks. Return to slow cooker; heat through. Spoon about 1/2 cup meat mixture in the center of each tortilla. Top with cheese, tomato, and sour cream. Fold ends and sides over filling. Enjoy!

Slow Cooker Stew

Ingredients

16 ounces lean beef stew meat, cubed
1/2 cup chopped onion
2 cups chopped carrots
1 1/2 cups chopped celery
4 cups diced raw potatoes
1 3/4 cups (one 15 ounce can) Swanson Beef Broth
1 tbsp. parsley flakes
1/2 tsp. Italian seasoning
1/8 tsp. black pepper
2 tbsp. Quick Cooking Minute Tapioca

Method

In a large skillet sprayed with butter flavored cooking spray, brown the meat. Spray a slow cooker container with cooking spray. Place the browned meat and add the onion, carrots, celery and potatoes. Mix well to combine. In a small bowl, combine beef broth, parsley flakes, Italian seasoning, black pepper, and uncooked tapioca. Pour mixture over vegetables. Cover and cook on LOW for 8 hours. Mix well before serving. Enjoy!

Slow Cooker Sweet and Sour Pork

Ingredients

1 1/2 pounds pork loins, lean, boneless, cut into cubes
8 ounces canned pineapple chunks in juice, undrained (unsweetened juice)
1 medium red bell pepper, cut into squares
3 tbsp. brown sugar [substitute w/Brown Sugar Twin or Splenda]
1/2 tsp. ginger
1/4 cup vinegar
3 tbsp. soy sauce
3 tbsp. water
2 tbsp. cornstarch
2 cups cooked rice

Method

In a 3-1/2 to 4 quart slow cooker, combine pork, pineapple, bell pepper, brown sugar, ginger, vinegar and soy sauce. Mix well. Cover; cook on LOW setting for 6 to 8 hours. About 5 minutes before serving, in small bowl, combine 3 tbsp. water and cornstarch; blend well. Stir into pork mixture in slow cooker. Cover; cook on high setting for an additional 5 minutes or until thickened. Serve pork mixture over rice. Prepare rice 25 minutes before serving. Enjoy!

Slow Cooker Tasty Mex Casserole

Ingredients

1 1/2 lb. lean ground beef
3 tbsp. white vinegar
1 tbsp. chili powder
1 tsp. dried whole oregano
1/4 tsp. garlic powder
1 1/2 tsp. Salt
1/4 tsp. Pepper
1 1/4 cups chopped onion
1 medium green pepper, chopped
4 oz. canned chopped green chilies, drained (optional)
12 oz. canned whole kernel corn, drained
1 cup elbow macaroni, partially cooked, drained and rinsed
2 (14 oz.) cans tomatoes with juice, broken up
2 tsp. chili powder
1 tsp. parsley flakes

1/2 tsp. dried whole oregano

2 tsp. granulated sugar

1/2 tsp. Salt

1/4 tsp. Pepper

Method

Mix first 7 ingredients in bowl. Scramble and fry in nonstick frying pan until browned. Drain and keep aside. Put the onion into a 3 1/2 or 5 quart slow cooker. Add green pepper, green chilies, corn and partially cooked macaroni. Add beef mixture. Stir. Combine remaining 7 ingredients in bowl. Stir well. Pour over the beef mix. Stir, cover and cook on LOW for 8 hours or on HIGH for 4 hours. Enjoy!

Slow Cooker Vegetable Minestrone

Ingredients

4 cups vegetable or chicken broth

4 cups tomato juice

1 tbsp. dried basil leaves

1 tsp. salt

1/2 tsp. dried oregano leaves

1/4 tsp. pepper

2 medium carrots, sliced

2 medium celery stalks, chopped

1 medium onion, chopped

1 cup sliced fresh mushrooms

2 garlic cloves, finely chopped

1 can diced tomatoes (28 ounces) undrained

1 1/2 cups uncooked rotini pasta

Shredded Parmesan if desired

Method

Mix all ingredients in a 4 – 5 quart slow cooker, except pasta and cheese. Cover and cook on low heat setting 7-8 hours or until veggies are tender. Stir in pasta, cover and cook on high heat setting 15-20 minutes or until pasta is tender. Sprinkle each serving with cheese. Enjoy!

Slow Cooker Wild Rice Soup

Ingredients

1/2 Cup Wild Rice

1/2 Cup Shredded Carrot

3 Cans Fat-free Chicken Broth

1 Pound Boneless Skinless Chicken Breast Halves, cut in 1" pieces

1/2 Cup Chopped Celery, approx. 1 stalk

1/2 Cup Chopped Onion, approx. 1 medium onion

8 Ounces Spinach Leaves, Whole

1 Cup Fat-free Sour Cream

1/2 Cup Flour

Method

Stir together all ingredients except spinach, sour cream and flour in slow cooker. Cover; cook on LOW for 10-12 hours or until chicken and rice are tender. Just before serving, stir together sour cream and flour in small bowl until smooth. Increase heat to HIGH and add the spinach and slowly stir sour cream mixture into hot soup mixture, stirring constantly. Cook, stirring occasionally, until soup is thickened and creamy (6 to 10 min.) Enjoy!

Slow Cooker Spicy Black-Eyed Peas

Ingredients

1 lb. dried black-eyed peas, sorted and rinsed
1 medium onion, chopped
6 cups water
1 tsp. salt
1/2 tsp. pepper
3/4 cup medium or hot salsa

Method

Mix all ingredients except salsa in 3 1/2 quart to 6 quart slow cooker. Cover and cook on high 3-4 hours or until peas are tender. Stir in salsa. Cover and cook on HIGH about 10 min. or until hot. Enjoy!

Smoky Ham and Navy Bean Stew

Ingredients

1 pound extra lean ham, cut into 1/2" cubes
2 cups water
1 cup dried navy beans
1 cup sliced celery
2 medium carrots, sliced
1/4 tsp. dried thyme leaves
1/4 tsp. liquid smoke flavoring
1/4 cup chopped fresh parsley

Method

In a 3-1/2 to 4 quart slow cooker, combine all ingredients except parsley; mix well. Cover and cook on low setting for 10 to 12 hours. Just before serving, stir in parsley. Enjoy!

Smoky Joe's Slow-Cooker Beef Stew

Ingredients

1 pound well-trimmed beef cubes
3/4 cup drained salsa
¾ cup barbecue sauce
1 (1.25-ounce) packet reduced-sodium taco seasoning mix
2 cups frozen corn
2 (15-ounce) cans rinsed and drained black beans
1 (19-ounce) can rinsed and drained chickpeas or garbanzo beans
1/2 cup fresh cilantro

Method

In a 3- or 4-quart slow cooker, combine the beef, salsa, barbecue sauce, taco mix and corn; mix well. Cover and cook on high for 3 to 4 hours or low for 6 to 8 hours, or until meat is tender. Add beans and cilantro; mix well. Cover and let stand 5 minutes for beans to heat through. Enjoy!

Smothered Chicken

Ingredients

4 whole boneless skinless chicken breasts
12 ounces Mushrooms
1 can 98% fat-free Cream of mushroom soup
1 can 98% fat-free Cream of chicken soup
1 can French Onion Soup

Method

Add all the ingredients into a crock pot and cook on low heat for about 10-12 hours. Serve over rice, noodles or potatoes. Enjoy!

Smothered Chicken with Pierogies

Ingredients

1 dozen frozen potato and cheddar cheese Pierogies
1 can (10 ¾ oz.) low fat cream of chicken soup
1 can (4 oz.) sliced mushrooms, drained
1 cup frozen peas
2 cups cubed or shredded cooked chicken

Method

Spray a 3 ½ to 4 quart slow cooker with some cooking spray. Add all the ingredients to the slow cooker and mix well. Cover and cook on low heat for 6-8 hours. Serve hot. Enjoy!

Smothered Steak

Ingredients

1 (1 1/2 lb.) lean boneless round tip steak
3 tbsp. all-purpose flour
1/4 tsp. Pepper
1 (14 1/2 oz.) package frozen chopped onion, celery, and pepper blend, thawed

2 tbsp. low-sodium Worcestershire sauce
1 tbsp. red wine vinegar
1/4 tsp. Salt
3 cups cooked long grain rice (cooked without salt or fat)

Method

Trim the fat from the steak and cut the steak into 1 1/2" pieces. Place the steak in a 4 quart electric slow cooker. Add flour and pepper; toss. Add tomato and next 4 ingredients and stir well. Cover and cook on HIGH 1 hr.; reduce heat to LOW and cook 7 hours or until steak is tender, stirring once. To serve, spoon evenly over 1/2 cup portions of rice. Enjoy!

Chop Suey over Rice

Ingredients

1 lb. boneless pork shoulder, cut into 3/4' cubes
1 small onion, cut into 1/4" wedges
1 (5 oz.) can sliced bamboo shoots, drained
1/2 cup purchased teriyaki baste and glaze
1 tsp. grated ginger root

1 (1 lb.) package frozen broccoli, carrots and water chestnuts, thawed, drained
2 cups uncooked instant white rice
2 cups water

Method

In a 4-6 quart slow cooker, combine first 6 ingredients; mix well. Cover and cook on LOW for 5-7 hours. About 15 minutes before serving, stir the vegetables into the pork. Increase the heat setting to high; cover and cook an additional 10-15 minutes or until vegetables are tender. Meanwhile, cook rice in water as directed on package. Serve the pork mixture over rice. Enjoy!

Colorful Chicken Stew

Ingredients

1 lb. boneless skinless chicken breasts, cubed
1 can 14 1/2 oz. Italian diced tomatoes, undrained
2 medium potatoes, peeled and cut into 1/2 inch cubes
5 medium carrots, chopped
3 celery ribs, chopped
1 large onion, chopped
2 cups cold water

1 medium green pepper, chopped
2 cans (4 oz. each) mushroom stems & pieces, drained
2 low-sodium chicken bouillon cubes
2 tsp. sugar (I used Splenda)
1 tsp. chili powder
1/4 tsp. pepper
1 tbsp. cornstarch

Method

In a 5 quart slow cooker, combine the first 12 ingredients. In a small bowl, combine the cornstarch and water until smooth. Stir into chicken mixture. Cover and cook on low for 8, 10 hours or until vegetables are tender. Serve hot. Enjoy!

Coq au Vin

Ingredients

4 slices thick-cut bacon
2 cups frozen pearl onions, thawed
1 cup button mushrooms, sliced
1 clove garlic, minced
1 tsp. dried thyme leaves
1/8 tsp. black pepper

2 pounds boneless skinless chicken breast halves, cut into 6, 5 oz. pieces
1 cup dry red wine
3/4 cup reduced-sodium chicken broth
1/4 cup tomato paste
3 tbsp. all-purpose flour

Method

Cook the bacon in medium skillet over medium heat. Drain and crumble. Layer ingredients in slow cooker in the following order: onions, bacon, mushrooms, garlic, thyme, pepper, chicken, wine and broth. Cover and cook on LOW 6 to 8 hours. Remove chicken and vegetables; cover and keep warm. Ladle 1 cup cooking liquid into small bowl; allow to cool slightly. Turn the slow cooker to HIGH; cover. Mix reserved liquid, tomato paste and flour until smooth. Return mixture to slow cooker; cover and cook 15 minutes or until thickened. Serve over egg noodles, if desired. Enjoy!

Corn, Ham and Potato Scallop

Ingredients

6 cups peeled baking potatoes, cut in 1" cubes
1 1/2 cups cubed cooked ham
1 (15.25oz.) can Green Giant Whole Kernel Sweet Corn, drained
1/4 cup chopped green bell pepper

2 tsp. instant minced onion
1 10 3/4oz.can condensed Cheddar Cheese Soup
1/2 cup milk
2 tbsp. all-purpose flour

Method

In a 3 1/2 to 4-quart Crock-Pot slow cooker, combine potatoes, ham, corn, bell pepper and onion; mix well. In a small bowl, combine soup, milk and flour; beat with wire whisk until smooth. Pour the soup mixture over the potato mixture; stir gently to mix. Cover; cook on low setting for 7-9 hours or until potatoes are tender. Enjoy!

Corned Beef Hash

Ingredients

3 cups corned beef brisket, cooked
2 small onions, chopped
3 potatoes, chopped
1 tsp. salt
1/2 tsp. pepper
1 cup low fat beef broth

Method

Run first three ingredients through food processor. Mix well with all the remaining ingredients. Press into well-greased pot. Cover and cook on LOW for 8 to 10 hours. Enjoy!

Creamy Red Potatoes

Ingredients

2 Pounds Red Potatoes – quartered
8 Ounces Neufchatel Cheese
10 3/4 Ounces Cream of Potato Soup
1 Envelope Ranch-style Dressing Mix

Method

Place potatoes in slow cooker. Beat together the cream cheese, soup and salad dressing mix. Pour onto the potatoes. Cover and cook on Low for 8 hours, or until potatoes are tender. Enjoy!

Creamy Red Potatoes and Chicken

Ingredients

1 1/2 Pounds Red Potatoes, cubed
8 Ounces Neufchatel Cheese
10 3/4 Ounces Cream of Potato Soup
1 Envelope Ranch-style Dressing Mix
12 Ounces Chicken Breast Without Skin, cut into strips

Method

Place potatoes in slow cooker. Beat together the cream cheese, soup and salad dressing mix. Stir in chicken strips and spread over potatoes (or just stir all together). Cover and cook on Low for 8 hours, or until potatoes are tender. Stir once after 5-6 hours. Stir before serving. Enjoy!

Crocked Pineapple Chicken

Ingredients

6 whole chicken breast halves without skin, skinned and split
1 dash pepper
Paprika, to taste
20 ounces pineapple chunks in juice
2 tbsp. Dijon mustard
2 tbsp. soy sauce

1 clove garlic, minced

Method

Arrange the chicken in the bottom of crockpot. Sprinkle with pepper and paprika. In a small bowl, combine the drained pineapple tidbits, mustard and soy sauce. Pour over chicken. Add minced garlic. Cover and cook on LOW 7-9 hours or HIGH 3-4 hours. Serve hot. Enjoy!

Crockpot Beef and Broth

Ingredients

2 tbsp. vegetable oil
2 pounds beef shank cross-cuts or soup bones
5 cups cold water
1 1/4 tsp. salt
1/4 tsp. dried thyme leaves
1 medium carrot, chopped

1 medium stalk celery with leaves, chopped
1 small onion, chopped
5 peppercorns
3 whole cloves
3 sprigs parsley
1 dried bay leaf

Method

Heat oil in 12-inch skillet over medium heat. Cook beef in oil until brown on both sides. Mix the remaining ingredients in a 3 1/2, 6 quart slow cooker. Add beef and cover and cook on low heat setting for 8 to 10 hours. Remove the beef from the broth and cool it for about 10 minutes or just until cool enough to handle. Strain the broth through a cheesecloth-lined sieve; discard vegetables and seasonings. Separate the beef from bones. Cut beef into 1/2-inch pieces. Skim fat from broth. Use immediately, or cover and refrigerate broth and beef in separate containers up to 24 hours or freeze for future use. Enjoy!

Crockpot Beef with Mushrooms & Red Wine Gravy

Ingredients

1 1/2 lbs. well-trimmed beef stew meat, cut into one inch cubes
2 medium onions cut into half inch wedges
1 package sliced fresh mushrooms
1 envelope beefy onion soup mix
3 tbsp. cornstarch
Salt & pepper to taste
1 1/2 cups dry red wine

Method

Place beef, onions and mushrooms in a 4-quart or larger slow cooker (crockpot). Add dry soup mix. Sprinkle with cornstarch and salt and pepper to taste. Pour wine over all. Cover and cook on low for 10 to 12 hours or on high for 5 to 6 hours. Stir well before serving. Enjoy!

Crockpot Big Bowl of Red Chili

Ingredients

3 small onion, chopped
1 green bell pepper, chopped
2 red bell peppers, chopped
4 cloves garlic, minced
2 jalapenos, seeded and minced
1 large tomato, chopped
56 ounces tomatoes, crushed

45 ounces kidney beans, drained and rinsed
2 tbsp. chili powder
2 tbsp. dried oregano
4 tsp. cumin
2 tsp. paprika
4 tsp. Tabasco sauce
1 tsp. ground black pepper

Method

Combine all ingredients in crockpot. Cook on low setting for 8-10 hours. Enjoy!

Crockpot Black Bean Soup

Ingredients

1/4 lb. chorizo
1 small onion, chopped
1 clove garlic, minced
1 small red pepper, chopped
1 small green pepper, chopped
2 tbsp. dry sherry
1 tsp. ground cumin

1 bay leaf
15 oz. can black beans, undrained
15 oz. can full fat chicken broth
juice of 1 lime
2 tbsp. minced cilantro
1/4 tsp. each salt and pepper

Method

Discard chorizo skin. Crumble meat and brown in a non-stick skillet for 2 minutes. Add onion, garlic, and peppers. Sauté over medium high heat 5 minutes. Add to slow cooker. Add sherry, cumin, bay leaf, beans and broth. Cover and cook on low for 4 to 5 hours. Remove lid. Scoop out 1 cup beans and press with the back of a fork to mash. Return to pot. Add lime juice, cilantro, salt and pepper. Simmer uncovered just to warm through, about 5 minutes. Enjoy!

Crockpot Chicken

Ingredients

1 10 3/4 oz. can Healthy Request Cream of Chicken Soup
1 package dry onion soup mix
2 Cups water
2 Cups uncooked instant rice

16 oz. skinless, boneless chicken breast, cut in 1" pieces
1 Cup sliced mushrooms
1/8 t black pepper

Method

Spray slow cooker with cooking spray. In prepared crockpot, combine first 4 ingredients. Add chicken, mushrooms, and pepper. Cover and cook on low 6-8 hours. Stir before serving. Enjoy!

Crock Pot Chicken #2

Ingredients

4-6 boneless skinless chicken breasts
1/4 cup white wine
1 package Italian salad dressing mix

Method

Brown chicken in a skillet and place in a crockpot. Sprinkle salad dressing mix over chicken. Add wine. Cover; cook on high about 4 hours. (Low for 6 – 8 hours.)

Crockpot Chicken & Stuffing

Ingredients

4 chicken breasts (halves)
1 package Stove Top Stuffing
1/2 cup water
1 can full fat cream of mushroom soup
1 cup chicken broth

Method

Place chicken on bottom of Crockpot. Pour broth over the chicken. Mix together the stuffing, soup, and water, and place on top of the chicken. Cook on low for 7 hours. Enjoy!

Crockpot Chicken Chili

Ingredients

6 skinless chicken thighs
1 large onion, chopped
2 cloves garlic, finely chopped
1 (14.5 oz.) can chicken broth
1 tsp. ground cumin
1 tsp. dried oregano leaves
1/2 tsp. salt

1/4 tsp. red pepper sauce
2 (15 oz.) cans great northern beans, rinsed and drained
1 (15 oz.) can white shoe peg corn, drained
3 tbsp. lime juice
2 tbsp. chopped fresh cilantro

Method

Remove the excess fat from chicken. Mix the onion, garlic, broth, cumin, oregano, salt and pepper sauce in 3 1/2 to 6 quart slow cooker. Add chicken. Cover and cook on low heat setting 4 to 5 hours or until chicken is tender. Remove chicken from slow cooker. Use 2 forks to remove bones and shred chicken into pieces. Discard bones; return chicken to slow cooker. Stir in the beans, corn, lime juice and cilantro. Cover and cook on low heat setting 15 to 20 minutes or until beans and corn are hot. Enjoy!

Crockpot Chicken Fajitas

Ingredients

7 boned and skinned chicken breast halves, cut in strips
2 onions, sliced
2 green bell peppers, cut in strips
2 red bell peppers, cut in strips
2 jalapeno chili pepper, chopped
8 flour tortillas

4 cloves garlic, minced
2 tsp. chili powder
2 tsp. ground cumin
2 tsp. ground coriander
28 ounces tomatoes, canned
1/4 cup water

Method

Combine all ingredients in crockpot. Cover and cook on low for 8-10 hours. Serve with salsa. Enjoy!

Crock Pot Chicken Marengo

Ingredients

10 oz. Canned sliced mushrooms, drained   1 cup Sliced onion

3 lbs. Chicken parts, skin removed
14 oz. Canned tomatoes with juice
(broken up)

1 x 1 ½ oz. Envelope Spaghetti sauce mix

Method

Arrange mushrooms and onion in 5 quart slow cooker. Layer the chicken pieces in the slow cooker. Stir the tomato and spaghetti sauce mix together in bowl. Pour on the chicken. Cover and cook on low for 8 to 10 hours or on High for 4 to 5 hours. Serve hot Enjoy!

Crockpot Chicken Paprika

Ingredients

12 oz. of chicken breast strips
3 cups of potatoes, sliced (skin left on, optional)
3 cups of onions, peeled and sliced

1 cup of water
Pam spray
Paprika, to taste

Method

Place 4 strips on bottom of pot and sprinkle with paprika. Then cover with a layer of potatoes. Cover the bacon with a layer of onions. Then spray Pam over this. Generously sprinkle with paprika. Then start over until you have made 4 layers. Pour the cup of water into the crockpot (down the side so as to not wash away the paprika).Cook on high all day and then enjoy. Enjoy!

Crockpot Chicken Tortilla Soup

Ingredients

1 1/2 lbs. boneless skinless chicken breasts, cooked and shredded
15 ounces whole tomatoes
10 ounces enchilada sauce
1 medium onion, chopped
4 ounces chopped green chilies
1 clove garlic, minced
2 cups water
14 1/2 ounces fat-free chicken broth
1 tsp. cumin
1 tsp. chili powder

1 tsp. salt
1/4 tsp. ground black pepper
1 whole bay leaf
6 whole corn tortillas
2 tbsp. vegetable oil
1 tbsp. chopped cilantro
Parmesan cheese, for garnish

Method

In an electric slow cooker, combine chicken, tomatoes, enchilada sauce, onion, green chilies and garlic. Add the water, broth, cumin, chili powder, salt, pepper and bay leaf. Mix well. Stir in corn and cover and cook on low 6 to 8 hours or on high 3 to 4 hours. Preheat oven to 400 degrees. Lightly brush both sides of tortillas with oil. Cut tortillas into 2 1/2-by- 1/2-inch strips. Place on a baking sheet. Bake, turning occasionally, until crisp, 5 to 10 minutes. Sprinkle tortilla strips, cilantro and Parmesan over soup. Enjoy!

Crockpot Chicken Tortilla Soup #2

Ingredients

16 ounces chicken breast halves without skin, cubed
30 ounces black beans, canned, undrained
30 ounces Mexican-style stewed tomatoes, canned
1 cup salsa
4 ounces chopped green chilies
14 1/2 ounces tomato sauce
2 cups reduced fat cheddar cheese
Tortilla Chips, a handful

Method

Combine all ingredients except cheese and tortilla chips into slow cooker. Cover and cook on low 8 hours. To serve, put a handful of chips into each individual bowl. Ladle soup over chips. Top with 1/4 cup cheese. Enjoy!

Crock-Pot Chili

Ingredients

1 pound ground round
1 cup chopped onion
1/2 cup chopped green bell pepper
1/4 cup dry red wine or water
1 tbsp. chili powder
1 tsp. tsp. sugar
1 tsp. tsp. ground cumin
1/4 tsp. salt
1 garlic clove, minced
1 15oz can kidney beans, drained

1 (14.5 0z.) can Mexican-style stewed tomatoes with jalapeno peppers and spices, undrained
6 tbsp. shredded reduced-fat extra-sharp cheddar cheese

Method

Cook the ground round in a large nonstick skillet over medium-high heat until brown, stirring to crumble. Add the chopped onion and the next 7 ingredients (onion through garlic), and cook for 7 minutes or until onion is tender. Place the meat mixture in an electric slow cooker, and stir in beans and tomatoes. Cover with lid, and cook on low-heat setting for 4 hours. Spoon into bowls; sprinkle with cheese. Enjoy!

Crockpot Colorful Chicken Stew

Ingredients

1 lb. boneless skinless chicken breasts, cubed
1 (14 1/2 oz.) can Italian diced tomatoes, undrained
2 medium potatoes, peeled and cut into 1/2-inch cubes
5 medium carrots, chopped
3 celery ribs, chopped
1 large onion, chopped

1 medium green bell pepper, chopped
2 (4 oz.) cans mushroom stems and pieces, drained
2 low-sodium chicken bouillon cubes
Artificial Sweetener equal to 2 tsp. Sugar
1 tsp. chili powder
1/4 tsp. pepper
1 tbsp. cornstarch
2 cup cold water

Method

In a 5-quart crockpot, combine the first 12 ingredients. In a small bowl, combine cornstarch and water until smooth. Stir into chicken mixture. Cover and cook on LOW for 8 to 10 hours or until vegetables are tender. Enjoy!

Crockpot Soup

Ingredients

1 whole green pepper or red, chopped
1 whole onion, chopped
16 ounces ground beef sirloin
14 1/2 ounces Chicken broth, Swanson, 100% Fat Free
15 1/2 ounces pinto beans, canned
15 ounces corn, canned
15 ounces pork and beans

1 ounce chili seasoning mix
29 ounces tomatoes, canned, chopped
3 ounces elbow macaroni

Method

Brown ground beef, green pepper and onion. Add all other ingredients except macaroni in a crockpot. Cook on low for 8 to 10 hours. 20 minutes before serving, add elbow macaroni. Cook until macaroni is tender. Serve hot. Enjoy!

Crock Pot Soup #1

Ingredients

1 can chicken broth
1 chopped onion
1 red bell pepper
1 can pinto beans
1 can corn, drained
1 can pork and beans
1 package chili seasoning mix
2 cans chopped tomatoes

Method

Put all ingredients in crock pot and simmer all day. Serve hot. Enjoy!

Crockpot Sour Cream Salsa Chicken

Ingredients

4 skinless boneless chicken breast halves
1 package reduced-sodium taco seasoning mix
1 cup salsa
2 tbsp. cornstarch
1/4 cup light sour cream

Method

Spray the crockpot with cooking spray. Add the chicken breasts. Sprinkle with Taco Seasoning. Top with salsa. Cook on low for 6-8 hours. When ready to serve, remove the chicken from the pot. Place about 2 tbsp. cornstarch in a small amount of water. Stir well. Stir the cornstarch mixture into salsa sauce. Stir in 1/4 cup of sour cream. Enjoy!

Crockpot Split Pea Soup

Ingredients

2 1/2 cups split peas
1 1/2 cups extra lean ham, diced
1 tbsp. reduced-calorie margarine
1 tbsp. oil
2 whole carrots, peeled and diced
1 medium potato, peeled and diced
1 whole onion, diced
4 cups water
2 cups fat-free chicken broth
Salt and pepper, to taste

Method

Sauté diced onion in butter and oil until golden. Place the onion and the rest of the ingredients in a crockpot, cover, cook on medium for 8-10 hours. Enjoy!

Crockpot Swiss Steak

Ingredients

3 tbsp. Gold Medal all-purpose flour
1 tsp. ground mustard
1/2 tsp. salt
1 1/2 pounds beef boneless round, tip or chuck steak, cut into 6 pieces
2 tbsp. vegetable oil
1 large onion, sliced
1 large bell pepper, sliced
1 14.5oz can diced tomatoes, undrained
2 cloves garlic, finely chopped

Method

Mix flour, mustard and salt. Coat the beef with the flour mixture. Heat oil in a 10-inch skillet over medium heat. Cook beef in oil for about 15 minutes, turning once, until brown. Place beef in a 3 1/2 to 6 quart slow cooker; top with onion and bell pepper. Mix tomatoes and garlic; pour over the beef and vegetables. Cover and cook on low heat setting 7 to 9 hours or until beef is tender. Enjoy!

Crockpot Tuscan Pasta

Ingredients

1 pound boneless skinless chicken breast, cut into 1" pieces

15 ounces red kidney beans, canned, rinsed and drained

15 ounces tomato sauce, canned

29 ounces Italian-style tomatoes, stewed, 2 (14 1/2 ounce) cans

4 1/2 ounces mushrooms, canned, drained

1 medium green bell pepper, chopped

1/2 cup chopped onion

1/2 cup chopped celery

4 cloves garlic – minced

1 cup water

1 tsp. dried Italian seasoning

6 ounces spaghetti, thin, uncooked, broken into halves

Method

Place all ingredients except spaghetti in crockpot. Cover and cook on low 4 hours or until vegetables are tender. Turn to high. Stir in spaghetti; cover. Stir again after 10 minutes. Cover and cook 45 minutes, or until pasta is tender. Enjoy!

Crockpot Vegetable Pasta

Ingredients

2 tsp. margarine

1 zucchini, 1/4" slice

1 yellow squash, 1/4" slice

2 carrots, thinly sliced

1 1/2 cups mushrooms, fresh, sliced

1 package broccoli, cuts

4 green onions, sliced

1 clove garlic, minced

2 egg yolk

1/2 tsp. basil, dried

1/4 tsp. salt

1/2 tsp. pepper

1 cup Parmesan Cheese, grated

12 ounces fettuccine

1 cup low fat mozzarella cheese, shredded

1 cup 2% low-fat milk

Method

Rub crock wall with butter. Put the zucchini, yellow squash, carrots, mushrooms, broccoli, onions, garlic, seasonings and Parmesan in the crock-pot. Cover and cook on High for 2 hours. Cook fettuccine according to package directions; drain. Add the cooked fettuccine, mozzarella, cream and egg yolks. Stir to blend well. Allow to heat for 15 to 30 minutes. Serve hot. Enjoy!

Cuban Black Beans

Ingredients

1 pound dried black beans, sorted and rinsed
1 cup onion, chopped
1 1/2 cups bell pepper, chopped
5 cloves garlic, finely chopped
14 1/2 ounces diced tomatoes, undrained

5 cups water
2 tbsp. olive oil, (or vegetable oil)
4 tsp. ground cumin
2 tsp. jalapeno chili pepper, finely chopped
1 tsp. salt
2 bay leaves, whole

Method

Combine all ingredients in crockpot. Cook on high for 6-8 hours. Remove bay leaves before serving. Serve over hot cooked rice. Garnish with diced hardboiled egg, hot sauce, and/or diced red onion. Enjoy!

Drunken Rosemary Chicken with Basmati Rice

Ingredients

8 chicken thighs
Salt and fresh-ground pepper, to taste
6 cloves garlic, peeled and thinly sliced
1 tsp. coarsely chopped fresh rosemary leaves or dried rosemary
1 cup Chardonnay or other dry white wine

1/2 cup fat-skimmed chicken broth
1 1/2 cups precooked dried white rice
1/4 cup chopped green onions (including tops)
Rosemary sprigs, rinsed

Method

Rinse thighs and pat dry. Pull off and discard skin; trim off and discard lumps of fat. Sprinkle thighs lightly with salt and pepper. Place thighs in a 4 1/2-quart or larger electric slow-cooker. Sprinkle the garlic and chopped rosemary; pour wine and broth over chicken. Cover and cook until meat pulls easily from the bone, about 5 hours on low or 3 hours on high. Skim and discard fat from juices. Add rice and mix to moisten evenly. Turn the cooker to high; cover and cook, stirring several times, until rice is just tender to bite, about 5 minutes. Spoon the chicken and rice onto a platter. Sprinkle with onions and garnish with rosemary sprigs. Add salt and pepper to taste. Enjoy!

Easiest Crock Pot Chicken

Ingredients

1 Package chicken breast halves
1 Can 98% fat-free cream of mushroom soup
1 Can 98% fat-free cream of chicken soup

Method

Skin chicken pieces (or use boneless, skinless chicken breasts). Place in crockpot. Mix together soups, and pour over chicken. Cook on low, all day. Remove chicken from sauce, remove bones. Serve over hot rice. Enjoy!

Easy Baked Beans

Ingredients

2 cans (28 oz. each) vegetarian baked beans, drained
1 medium onion, chopped
2/3 cup barbecue sauce
1/2 cup packed brown sugar
2 tbsp. ground mustard (dry)

Method

Mix all ingredients in a 3 1/2 to 6 quart slow cooker. Cover and cook on LOW for 4 to 5 hours (or HIGH 2 2 1/2 hour) or until desired consistency is achieved. Serve hot. Enjoy!

Easy Cassoulet

Ingredients

8 ounces skinless boneless chicken thighs
2 medium carrots, cut in 1/2" pieces
1 medium red or green sweet pepper, cut in 1/2" pieces
1 cup onions, chopped
3 cloves garlic, minced
30 ounces white kidney beans or great northern, rinsed and drained

14 1/2 ounces Italian-style stewed tomatoes, undrained
8 ounces smoked turkey sausage, fully cooked – halved lengthwise & cut in 1/2" slices
1 1/2 cups dry white wine or chicken broth
1 tbsp. parsley, fresh, snipped
1 tsp. thyme, dried, crushed
1/4 tsp. ground red pepper

1 bay leaf

Method

Rinse chicken; pat dry. Cut chicken into 1" pieces. Place carrots, sweet pepper, onion, garlic, beans, tomatoes, chicken, and sausage in a 3 1/2, 4 or 5 quart crockery cooker. Combine the chicken broth or wine, parsley, thyme, red pepper, and bay leaf in a bowl. Add to crock cooker and cover and cook on low heat setting for 7 to 8 hours or on high heat setting for 3 1/2 to 4 hours. Discard bay leaf. Serve hot. Enjoy!

Easy Hearty Turkey Chili

Ingredients

1 large onion
2 cloves garlic
½ lb. ground turkey
2 tbsp. chili powder
1 tbsp. paprika
1 tsp. ground cumin
2 tbsp. crushed cherry peppers
2 tomatoes, chopped
1 cup fat free chicken broth
1 ½ tbsp. cider vinegar
2 cups kidney beans
1 green bell pepper

Method

Toss everything into a crock-pot and cook for 2 hours on high or 4 hours on low. Serve with baked tortilla chips. Enjoy!

Easy Italian Vegetable Soup

Ingredients

14 1/2 ounces diced tomatoes, undrained
10 1/2 ounces condensed beef broth, undiluted
8 ounces sliced mushrooms
1 medium zucchini, thinly sliced
1 medium green bell pepper, chopped
1 medium yellow onion, chopped
1/3 cup dry red wine, OR 1/3 cup beef broth
1 1/2 tbsp. dried basil leaves
2 1/2 tsp. sugar
1 tbsp. extra-virgin olive oil
1/2 tsp. salt

4 ounces shredded mozzarella cheese,
optional

Method

Combine the tomatoes, broth, mushrooms, zucchini, bell pepper, onion, wine, basil and sugar in slow cooker. Cook on LOW 8 hours or on HIGH 4 hours. Stir oil and salt into soup. Garnish with cheese, if desired. Makes 5 to 6 servings. Enjoy!

Eight Layer Casserole

Ingredients

1/2 lb. lean ground beef
2 tbsp. imitation bacon bits
1 small onion, chopped
1 (15 oz.) can tomato sauce
1/2 cup water
1/2 tsp. chili powder

1/4 tsp. Salt
1/4 tsp. ground black pepper
2/3 cup long-grain rice
1 (8 3/4 oz.) can whole-kernel corn, drained
1/2 cup chopped green bell pepper

Method

Crumble the beef evenly over bottom of a 3 1/2 quart slow cooker. Sprinkle the bacon bits and onion. In a medium bowl, combine the tomato sauce, water, chili powder, salt and black pepper; pour half over beef and onion layers. Sprinkle rice evenly over top, then corn. Top with remaining tomato sauce mixture, then bell pepper. Cover and cook on LOW about 5 hours or until rice is tender. Enjoy!

Family Favorite Chili

Ingredients

2 lbs. ground beef
1 large onion, chopped
2 cloves garlic, finely chopped
1 can (28 oz.) diced tomatoes, undrained
11 can (15 oz.) tomato sauce
2 tbsp. chili powder

1 1/2 tsp. ground cumin
1/2 tsp. salt
1/2 tsp. pepper
1 can (15 or 16 oz.) kidney or pinto beans, rinsed and drained

Method

Cook beef in 12" skillet over medium heat, stirring occasionally, until brown; drain. Mix beef and remaining ingredients except beans in 3 1/2 to 6 quarts slow cooker. Cover and cook on LOW 6 to 8 hours (or HIGH 3 to 4 hours) or until the onion is tender. Stir in the beans. Cover and cook on HIGH for 15-20 minutes or until slightly thickened. Enjoy!

Forgotten Minestrone

Ingredients

1 pound round steak, cut in 2" pieces., lean
6 cups water
1 (28 oz.) can canned tomatoes, cut up, undrained
2 beef bouillon cubes
1 medium onions, chopped
2 tbsp. dried parsley
1/2 tsp. salt – optional

1 1/2 tsp. thyme
1/2 tsp. pepper
1 medium zucchini, thinly sliced
1 (16 oz.) can garbanzo beans, rinsed & drained
1 cup elbow macaroni, or small shells
1/4 cup grated Parmesan cheese – optional

Method

In a slow cooker, combine the beef, water, tomatoes, bouillon, onion, parsley, salt if desired, thyme and pepper. Cover and cook on low for 7-9 hours or until meat is tender. Add zucchini, cabbage, beans and macaroni; cook on high, covered, 30-45 minutes more, or until the vegetables are tender. Sprinkle individual servings with Parmesan cheese if desired. Enjoy!

Frankfurters with Macaroni and Cheese

Ingredients

4 cups cooked elbow macaroni, rinsed and drained
1 1/2 cups (1 12 fluid once can) Carnation Evaporated Skim Milk
1 cup skim milk
2 tbsp. dried onion flakes

1 tsp. dried parsley flakes
2 cups (8 ounces) shredded Kraft reduced-fat Cheddar cheese
8 ounces Healthy Choice 97 percent fat-free frankfurters, diced

Method

In a slow cooker sprayed with butter-flavored cooking spray, combine macaroni, evaporated skim milk, skim milk, onion flakes and parsley flakes. Add Cheddar cheese and frankfurters. Mix well to combine. Cover and cook on low for 3 to 4 hours. Mix well before serving. Enjoy!

Garlic Pork Roast

Ingredients

3 1/2 pounds pork boneless loin roast
1 tbsp. vegetable oil
1 tsp. salt
1/2 tsp. pepper

1 medium onion, sliced
3 cloves garlic, peeled
1 cup fat-free chicken broth or water

Method

Trim excess fat from pork. Heat oil in 10 inch skillet over medium high heat and cook pork in oil about 10 minutes turning occasionally, until brown on all sides. Sprinkle with salt and pepper. Place onion and garlic in 3 ½ to 6 quart slow cooker. Place pork on the onion and garlic. Pour broth over pork. Cover and cook on low heat setting for 8-10 hours or until pork is tender. Enjoy!

Glow Pork Chops

Ingredients

5 whole pork loin chops, (5 to 6)
1/4 cup brown sugar
1/2 tsp. ground cinnamon
1/4 tsp. ground cloves

8 ounces tomato sauce
29 ounces peach halves
1/4 cup vinegar
Salt and pepper, to taste

Method

Lightly brown pork chops on both sides in a skillet and pour off the excess fat. Combine sugar, cinnamon, cloves, tomato sauce, 1/4 cup syrup from peaches, and vinegar. Sprinkle chops with salt and pepper. Arrange chops in crockpot. Place drained peach halves on top. Pour tomato mixture over all. Cover and cook 4 to 6 hours. Enjoy!

Ginger Pork Wraps

Ingredients

3 tbsp. grated ginger root
3 tbsp. honey
2 1/2 pounds boneless pork loin roast, trimmed of fat
1/4 cup hosin sauce
3 cups purchased coleslaw blend

2 tbsp. rice vinegar
12 whole fat-free flour tortilla, (8-10") heated

Method

In 3 1/2 to 4 quart slow cooker, combine the ginger root and honey; blend well. Add pork roast; turn to coat with honey mixture. Cover and cook on low setting for 6-8 hours. Remove the roast from the slow cooker. With 2 forks, shred pork; return to slow cooker. Stir in the hoisin sauce. In a medium bowl, combine coleslaw blend and vinegar; toss to mix well. To serve, spread about 1/3 cup pork mixture in the center of each warm tortilla. Top each with 1/4 cup coleslaw mixture. Roll up each tightly. Enjoy!

Ham and Potatoes au Gratin

Ingredients

2 full cups diced extra-lean ham
4 cups diced raw potatoes
1 cup chopped onion
3/4 cup shredded reduced-fat Cheddar Cheese

1 (10 3/4 ounce) can Healthy Request Cream of Celery Soup
1/8 tsp. black pepper
1 tsp. dried parsley flakes
1 tsp. prepared yellow mustard

Method

Spray a slow cooker with butter flavored cooking spray. Combine ham, potatoes and onion. Sprinkle Cheddar cheese evenly over top. In a small bowl, combine celery soup, black pepper, parsley flakes, and mustard. Add soup mixture to potato mixture. Mix well to combine. Cover and cook on LOW for 8 hours. Mix well before serving. Enjoy!

Hamburger and Noodle Soup

Ingredients

1 lb. lean or extra-lean ground beef
1 medium onion, coarsely chopped
1 stalk celery, cut into 1/4" slices
1 (1.15 oz.) package dry beefy mushroom soup mix
1 (14.5 oz.) can diced tomatoes, undrained
3 cups water
1/2 tsp. Salt

1/4 tsp. Pepper
2 cups frozen mixed vegetables, thawed and drained
2 oz. (1 cup) uncooked fine egg noodles

Method

Brown ground beef in large skillet until thoroughly cooked, stirring frequently. Drain well. In 4-6 quart slow cooker, combine cooked ground beef and all remaining ingredients except mixed vegetables and noodles; mix well. Cover; cook on LOW for 6-8 hrs. About 20 min. before serving, add thawed vegetables and egg noodles to soup; mix well. Increase heat setting to HIGH; cover and cook an additional 15-20 min. or until vegetables are crisp-tender and noodles are tender. Enjoy!

Ham Potluck Bake

Ingredients

1 1/2 cups shredded carrots
6 cups (20 oz.) shredded frozen potatoes
9 oz. (full 1/2 cups) Diced Dubuque 97% fat-free ham or any extra-lean
1 tbsp. dried onion flakes

1 (10 3/4 oz.) can Healthy Request Cream of Mushroom Soup
1/4 cup skim milk
1/8 tsp. black pepper
3/4 cup (3 oz.) shredded Kraft reduced-fat Cheddar cheese

Method

In a slow cooker container, combine carrots, potatoes, ham, and onion flakes. Add mushroom soup, skim milk, black pepper, and Cheddar cheese. Mix well to combine. Cover and cook on LOW for 6 to 8 hours. Stir well before serving. Enjoy!

Hearty Italian Spaghetti Dinner

Ingredients

12 ounces pork loin, lean, boneless, trimmed of fat, cut into 1x 1/4" strips
1 cup onion, finely chopped
1/2 cup sun-dried tomatoes, chopped
1 tbsp. dried parsley
1 tbsp. dried Italian seasoning
1/2 tsp. salt
4 cloves garlic, minced
28 ounces crushed tomatoes, with puree, undrained
8 ounces tomato sauce
12 ounces spaghetti, uncooked

Method

In a 3-1/2 or 4 quart Crock-Pot Slow Cooker, combine all ingredients except the spaghetti and mix well. Cover and cook on low setting for at least 7 hours or until the pork is no longer pink and onions are tender. Cook spaghetti to desired doneness as directed on the package. Drain. Serve pork mixture over the spaghetti. Enjoy!

Hearty Meatball Chowder

Ingredients

1 cup water
2 cans tomato soup
1 1/2 cups potatoes, diced
1 can diced tomatoes
11 1/2 ounces vegetable juice
1 can corn, whole kernel
1 can green beans, cut
1/2 tsp. thyme, dried
1/4 tsp. pepper
1 pound ground beef, extra lean
1 tsp. garlic, minced

Method

Mix the beef and garlic. Make 1/2" meat balls & brown in a skillet. Place the meatballs and all other ingredients in crockpot and set on low for 6-8 hours. Enjoy!

Herbed Turkey and Wild Rice Casserole

Ingredients

6 slices bacon, cut into 1/2" pcs.
1 lb. turkey breast tenderloin, cut into 3/4" pcs.
1 medium onion, chopped (1/2 cup)
1 medium carrot, sliced (1/2 cup)
1 medium stalk celery, sliced (1/2 cup)
2 cans (14 1/2 oz. each) ready-to-serve chicken broth
1 can (10 3/4 oz.) condensed cream of chicken soup
1/4 tsp. dried marjoram leaves
1/8 tsp. pepper
1 1/4 cups uncooked wild rice, rinsed and drained

Method

Cook bacon in 10" skillet over medium heat, stirring occasionally, until turkey is brown. Stir in onion, carrot and celery. Cook, 2 minutes, stirring occasionally; drain. Beat 1 can of the broth and the soup together in a 3 1/2 quart slow cooker, using wire whisk, until smooth. Stir in the remaining can of broth, the marjoram and pepper. Stir the turkey mixture and wild rice. Cover and cook on HIGH 30 min. Reduce heat to LOW. Cook 6-7 hours or until rice is tender and liquid is absorbed. Enjoy!

Herbed Turkey Breast

Ingredients

1 turkey breast, boneless and skinless
2 tbsp. butter or margarine (change to light butter)
1/4 cup garden vegetable flavored cream cheese (probably could get light/full fat)
1 tbsp. low sodium soy sauce
1 tbsp. fresh parsley, minced
1/2 tsp. basil, dried
1/2 tsp. sage, dried
1/2 tsp. thyme, dried
1/4 tsp. ground black pepper
1/4 tsp. garlic powder

Method

Place turkey in a slow cooker. Combine remaining ingredients and brush over the turkey. Cover and cook on low for 10 to 12 hours or high for 5 to 6 hours. Makes 8 servings. Enjoy!

Hot Crab Dip

Ingredients

1/2 cup skim milk
1/3 cup salsa
3 packages (8 oz. each) light cream cheese, cubed

2 packages (8 oz. each) imitation crab meat, flaked
1 cup thinly sliced green onions
1 can (4 oz.) chopped green chilies

Method

Combine the milk and salsa. Transfer to a slow cooker coated with nonstick cooking spray. Stir in the cream cheese, crab, onions and chilies. Cover and cook on LOW for 3-4 hours, stirring every 30 min. Enjoy!

Hot Fudge Crockpot Cake

Ingredients

3 cups skim milk
1 box sugar free cook and serve chocolate pudding
1 box Super Moist chocolate fudge cake mix
1 1/3cupwater
1/2cupapplesauce
6 egg whites

Method

Spray a crockpot container with nonfat cooking spray. Whisk skim milk with dry pudding mix in crockpot until dissolved. In a medium bowl, mix dry cake mix, water, applesauce and egg whites with whisk for two minutes until blended. Very gently pour cake mixture over pudding mixture. DO NOT MIX! Cover and cook on HIGH for 2 1/2 hours. Serve hot Enjoy!

Hot Texas Chili Soup

Ingredients

12 ounces red kidney beans, cooked and drained
6 ounces ground turkey, cooked
3 cups canned stewed tomatoes, low-sodium
2 cups tomato sauce
1 1/2 cups chopped onions
1 cup canned green chilies, rinsed, drained and chopped
1 tbsp. + 2 tsp. chili powder
1 1/2 tsp. ground cumin
1 tsp. paprika
1 tsp. dried oregano
1/4 tsp. hot pepper sauce

Method

In a 3-quart slow-cooker, combine all ingredients and 2 cups water. Cover and cook on Low for 4 hours or on High for 2 hours, until the onions are tender. Ladle evenly into 6 soup bowls. Serve hot. Enjoy!

Hungarian Goulash

Ingredients

2 tbsp. vegetable oil
2 pounds beef stew meat cut into inch pieces
1 large onion sliced
14 1/2 ounces fat-free beef broth
6 ounces tomato paste
2 cloves garlic finely chopped
1 tbsp. Worcestershire Sauce

1 tbsp. paprika
1 tsp. salt
1/4 tsp. caraway seeds, if desired
1/4 tsp. pepper
1/4 cup cold water
3 tbsp. all-purpose flour
1 medium bell pepper cut into strips
8 cups hot cooked noodles for serving

Method

Heat oil in a 10 inch skillet over medium high heat. Cook beef in oil for about 10 minutes, stirring occasionally until brown; drain. Place beef and onion in a 3 1/2 to 6 quart slow cooker. Mix broth, tomato paste, garlic, Worcestershire Sauce, paprika, salt, caraway seed and pepper; stir into beef mixture. Cover and cook on low heat setting for 8-10 hours or until the beef is tender. Mix water and flour; gradually stir into beef mixture. Stir in the bell pepper. Cover and cook on high heat setting 30 minutes. Serve goulash over noodles. Enjoy!

Slow Cooker Barbecued Turkey and Vegetables

Ingredients

1 cup barbecue sauce
1/2 cup hot water
2 turkey thighs (2 lb.), skin removed, cut in half
3 medium potatoes, unpeeled, cut into 8 pcs. Each
6 medium carrots, cut into 2 1/2x 1/2" sticks

Method

In a medium bowl, combine barbecue sauce and water; mix well. Layer the turkey, potatoes and carrots in a 3 1/2-4 quart slow cooker. Pour the sauce mixture over top. Cover and cook on LOW for at least 9 hours. Remove turkey and vegetables with slotted spoon; place on serving platter. Serve with cooking juices poured over the turkey and vegetables. Enjoy!

Slow Cooker BBQ Short Ribs

Ingredients

2 tbsp. cooking oil
3 lbs. beef short ribs
1 cup BBQ sauce
2 tbsp. Molasses
2 tbsp. white vinegar
1 1/2 tsp. Salt
1/2 tsp. Pepper
1 tbsp. soy sauce
1/2 cup chopped onion

Method

Heat cooking oil in frying pan and add the ribs and brown on all sides. Drain. Place the ribs in 5 quart slow cooker. Mix next 6 ingredients well in bowl. Stir in the onion. Pour over short ribs. Cook on LOW for 8-10 hours or on HIGH for 4 to 5 hours. Enjoy!

Slow Cooker Beef Short Ribs

Ingredients

4 lbs. beef short ribs, trimmed of fat
Salt, to taste
Pepper, to taste
2 medium onions, sliced or chopped
2 tsp. beef bouillon powder
1/2 tsp. liquid gravy browner
1 1/2 cups warm water

Method

Sprinkle short ribs with salt and pepper. Place the onion in bottom of 5 quart slow cooker. Arrange ribs over top. Stir bouillon powder and gravy browner into warm water. Pour over ribs. Cover and cook on LOW for 7-9 hours or on HIGH for 3 1/2-4 1/2 hours. Enjoy!

Slow Cooker Brunswick Stew

Ingredients

1 1/2 lbs. skinless, boneless chicken breasts, cut into 1" pcs.
3 medium potatoes, cut into 1/2" pcs.
1 medium carrot, chopped
1 can (28 oz.) crushed tomatoes, undrained
1 can (15 to 16 oz.) lima beans, rinsed and drained

1 can (14 3/4 oz.) cream-style corn
1 tbsp. Worcestershire sauce
3/4 tsp. Salt
1/2 tsp. dried marjoram leaves
8 slices bacon, cooked and crumbled
1/4 tsp. red pepper sauce

Method

Mix all ingredients except bacon and red pepper sauce in a 3 1/2-6 quart slow cooker. Cover and cook on LOW 8-10 hours (or HIGH 3-4 hours) or until potatoes are tender. Stir in the bacon and pepper sauce. Serve hot. Enjoy!

Slow Cooker-Creole Jambalaya

Ingredients

1 cup chopped onion
1 cup green bell pepper, chopped
1 cup chopped celery
3 cloves finely chopped garlic
1 (28 oz.) can undrained diced tomatoes
2 cups fully cooked smoked sausage, copped

1/2 tsp. parsley flakes
1/2 tsp. Salt
1/4 tsp. dried thyme leaves
1/4 tsp. red pepper sauce
3/4 lb. uncooked peeled deveined medium shrimp, thawed if frozen
4 cups hot cooked rice

Method

Mix all the ingredients except shrimp and rice in 3 1/2-6 quart slow cooker. Cover and cook on low 7-8 hours or until vegetables are tender. Stir in shrimp. Cover and cook on low about 30 min. or until shrimp are pink and firm. Serve with rice. Enjoy!

Slow Cooker Chicken Merlot

Ingredients

3 cups fresh mushrooms, sliced
1 onion, chopped

2 cloves garlic, minced

3 lbs. skinless chicken pieces, breasts, thighs, drumsticks, rinsed
3/4 cup chicken stock
6 ounces tomato paste
1/4 cup dry red wine, such as Merlot, or chicken stock

2 tbsp. quick cooking tapioca
2 tsp. Sugar
1-1/2 tsp. dried basil, crushed, or 2 tbsp. fresh, snipped
2 cups cooked noodles
2 tbsp. grated Parmesan cheese

Ingredients

Combine first 3 ingredients and salt and pepper to taste in a 3-1/2 to 5 quart slow cooker. Arrange the chicken pieces over vegetables. Combine the stock, next 4 ingredients and salt and pepper to taste in a bowl. Add dried basil if using. Pour over chicken. Cover and cook on low for 7-8 hours or on high for about 4 hours. Stir in fresh basil now if using. Serve noodles, sprinkled with parmesan cheese. Enjoy!

Slow-Cooker Chili Soup

Ingredients

1 tbsp. oil
1 1/2 pounds boneless beef round steak, cut into 1/2" cubes
1 1/2 cups water
1 cup onions, chopped
1 cup bell pepper, chopped
1/2 tsp. salt
1/2 tsp. pepper
1/2 tsp. cayenne pepper
1/4 tsp. garlic powder
29 ounces diced peeled tomatoes
15 1/2 ounces tomato sauce
1 cup carrots, chopped
31 ounces dark red kidney beans, drained

Method

After beef is browned in skillet, pour into slow-cooker with vegetables and spices. Cook for 4 to 5 hours on low setting until done. Serve hot. Enjoy!

Desserts & Beverages

Apples 'N Port

Ingredients

4 whole cooking apples
½ cup raisins or currants
1 cup brown sugar

1/4 teaspoon nutmeg
1/4 teaspoon ground cinnamon
2/3 cup port wine

Method

Core the apples and cut a score around the sides about 1/3 down from the top. Fill score with raisins or currants, and top with brown sugar, pressing the sugar lightly toward the center of the fruit. Place apples in the bottom of the crock pot, and pour port over them, seeing that some goes into each apple center. Cover and cook at Low for 3 to 4 hours, or until apples are soft. Serve with excess port sauce poured over apples.

Note: These apples are excellent hot or cold, and especially good served with rich vanilla ice cream or whipped cream. Enjoy!

Apple Pie Bread Pudding

Ingredients

12 slices reduced-calorie white bread, torn into medium-size pieces
3 1/2 cups cooking apples, cored, peeled and chopped
1 cup unsweetened apple juice
1/2 cup diet lemon-lime soda
Sugar substitute suitable for baking equal to 1/2 cup sugar
1 1/2 tsp. apple pie spice

Method

Spray a slow cooker with butter-flavored nonstick cooking spray. Combine the bread pieces and apples in slow cooker. In small bowl, combine apple juice, soda, sugar substitute and apple pie spice. Drizzle evenly over bread mixture. Mix gently to combine. Cover and cook for 6 hours on low, or until done. Mix well before serving. Enjoy!

Apple Butter

Ingredients

12 medium Granny Smith or other cooking apples, peeled and cut into fourths
1 1/2 cups packed brown sugar
1/2 cup apple juice

1 tsp. ground allspice
1 tsp. ground nutmeg
1/2 tsp. ground cloves

Method

Mix all ingredients in 5-6 quart slow cooker. Cover and cook on LOW 8-10 hours or until apples are very tender. Mash apples with potato masher or large fork. Cook uncovered on LOW for 1 to 2 hours, stirring occasionally, until the mixture is very thick. Cool for about 2 hours Spoon apple butter into container. Cover and store in refrigerator up to 3 weeks. Enjoy!

Cherry Cobbler

Ingredients

1 can (21 oz.) cherry pie filling
1 cup all-purpose flour
1/4 cup sugar
1/4 cup margarine or butter, melted

1/2 cup milk
1 tsp. baking powder
1/2 tsp. almond extract
1/4 tsp. salt

Method

Spray inside of a 2 -3 1/2 quart slow cooker with cooking spray. Pour the pie filling into cooker. Beat the remaining ingredients with spoon until smooth. Spread batter over pie filling. Cover and cook on HIGH 1 1/2 to 2 hours or until toothpick inserted in center comes out clean. Enjoy!

Crockpot Apple Pie

Ingredients

8 apples, tart, peeled and sliced
1 1/4 tsp. cinnamon
1/4 tsp. allspice
1/4 tsp. nutmeg
3/4 cup skim milk

2 tbsp. Brummel and Brown Spread – softened
3/4 cup Splenda
1/2 cup egg substitute
1 tsp. vanilla extract
1 1/2 cup Reduced Fat Bisquick

1/3 cup brown sugar   3 tbsp. cold butter

Method

Toss the apples in large bowl with cinnamon, allspice, and nutmeg. Place in a lightly greased crockpot. Combine the milk, softened butter, sugar, eggs, vanilla, and the 1/2 cup Bisquick. Spoon over apples. Combine the 1 cup Bisquick and brown sugar. Mix the cold butter into mixture until crumbly. Sprinkle this mixture over top of apple mixture. Cover and cook on low 6-7 hours or until apples are soft. Enjoy!

Pear Streusel

Ingredients

1/3 cup crunchy nutlike cereal nuggets
3 tbsp. all-purpose flour
3 tbsp. light brown sugar
2 tbsp. soft reduced-fat margarine
1 tsp. grated lemon peel

1/2 tsp. ground ginger
4 Bartlett pears, peeled, cored, and cut into 1/2" slices
3 tbsp. fresh lemon juice
1/4 cup granulated sugar

Method

In a small bowl, combine cereal, flour, brown sugar, margarine, lemon peel and ginger. Mix with a fork until the mixture is crumbly; set aside. In a 1 quart casserole dish that fits into a 4 or 5 quart slow cooker, combine pears, lemon juice, and granulated sugar. Sprinkle crumb mixture evenly over top. Place casserole in slow cooker. Cover and cook on HIGH 2 hours or until pears are fork tender. Serve warm. Enjoy!

Chocolate-Coffee Cake

Ingredients

6 tbsp. margarine or butter, room temperature
1 1/3 cups sugar
2 eggs
1 cup all-purpose flour
1/3 cup Dutch process cocoa

1/2 tsp. baking soda
1/4 tsp. each: baking powder, salt
1–2 tbsp. instant espresso or coffee mixed with boiling water
1/3 cup reduced-fat sour cream
Coffee Glaze (recipe follows)

Method

Beat the margarine and sugar in a bowl until fluffy; beat in eggs one at a time, beating well after each addition. Mix in combined dry ingredients alternately with a mixture of espresso, boiling water, and sour cream, beginning and ending with dry ingredients. Pour the batter into greased and floured 6-cup fluted cake pan; place pan on rack in 6-quart slow cooker. Cover and cook on high until toothpick inserted in center of cake comes out clean, 4 to 41/2 hours. Cool cake on wire rack 10 minutes; invert cake onto rack and cool. Drizzle cake with Coffee Glaze. Enjoy!

Coffee Glaze

Makes about 1/3 cup

Ingredients
3/4 cup powdered sugar
1 tbsp. margarine or butter, melted
2–3 tbsp. strong brewed coffee

Method

Mix the powdered sugar, margarine, and enough coffee to make glaze consistency. Enjoy!

Flourless Mocha Mousse Cake

Ingredients

1/2 cup Dutch process cocoa
3/4 cup packed light brown sugar
3 tbsp. flour
2 tsp. instant espresso powder
1/8 tsp. salt
3/4 cup 2% reduced-fat milk
1 tsp. vanilla

2 ounces semi-sweet chocolate, chopped
2 ounces bittersweet chocolate, chopped
1 egg
3 egg whites
1/8 tsp. cream of tartar
1/3 cup granulated sugar
Cocoa or powdered sugar, as garnish

Method

Combine the cocoa, brown sugar, flour, espresso powder, and salt in a medium saucepan; gradually whisk in milk and vanilla to make smooth mixture. Whisk over medium heat until mixture is hot and sugar dissolved (do not boil). Remove the saucepan from heat; add the chocolate, whisking until melted. Whisk about 1/2 cup chocolate mixture into egg; whisk egg mixture back into saucepan. Cool to room temperature. Beat the egg whites and cream of tartar to soft peaks; beat to stiff peaks, gradually adding granulated sugar. Stir about 1/4 of the egg whites into cooled chocolate mixture; fold chocolate mixture into remaining egg whites. Pour the batter into lightly greased 7-inch spring form pan; place on rack in 6-quart slow cooker. Cover, placing 3 layers of paper toweling under lid, and cook on high until toothpick inserted 1/2-inch from edge of cake comes out clean (cake will look moist and will be soft in the center), for 2 1/4 to 3 1/4 hours. Remove the pan to wire rack and cool completely; refrigerate, loosely covered, 8 hours or overnight. Remove side of pan and place cake on serving plate; sprinkle top of cake generously with cocoa. Enjoy!

Chocolate Sauerkraut Cake

Ingredients

3/4 cup sugar
1/4 cup vegetable shortening
1 egg
1 tsp. vanilla
1/4 cup unsweetened cocoa
1 cup plus 2 tbsp. all-purpose flour

1/2 tsp. each: baking powder, baking soda
1/4 tsp. salt
1/2 cup beer or water
1/3 cup finely chopped sauerkraut, well-drained, rinsed
Chocolate Glaze (recipe follows)

Method

Beat the sugar and shortening in large bowl until blended; beat in the egg, vanilla, and cocoa. Mix in a mixture of the flour, baking powder, baking soda, and salt alternately with beer, beginning and ending with dry ingredients. Mix in the sauerkraut. Pour the batter into greased and floured 6-cup fluted cake pan; place on rack in 6-quart slow cooker. Cover and cook on high until toothpick inserted in center of cake comes out clean, 2 1/2 to 3 hours. Cool cake on wire rack 10 minutes; invert onto rack and cool. Drizzle Chocolate Glaze over. Enjoy!

Chocolate Glaze

Makes about 1/3 cup

Ingredients

3/4 cup powdered sugar
2 tbsp. unsweetened cocoa
1/2 tsp. vanilla
Milk

Method

Mix the powdered sugar, cocoa, vanilla, and enough milk to make glaze consistency. Enjoy!

Chocolate Zucchini Cake

Ingredients

1/4 cup each: room temperature margarine or butter, applesauce
3/4 cup sugar
1 egg
1/4 cup low-fat buttermilk
1 tsp. vanilla
11/4 cups all-purpose flour

2 tbsp. unsweetened cocoa
1/2 tsp. each: baking soda, baking powder
1/4 tsp. each: salt, ground cinnamon and cloves
1 cup finely chopped or shredded zucchini
1/4 cup semisweet chocolate morsels
Powdered sugar, as garnish

Method

Beat margarine, applesauce, and sugar in large bowl until smooth. Mix in the egg, buttermilk, and vanilla. Mix in the combined flour, cocoa, baking soda, baking powder, salt, and spices; mix in the zucchini and chocolate morsels. Pour the batter into greased and floured 6-cup fluted cake pan; place pan on rack in 6-quart slow cooker. Cover and cook on high until toothpick inserted in center of cake comes out clean, for 3 to 4 hours. Cool cake on wire rack 10 minutes; invert cake onto rack and cool. Sprinkle generously with powdered sugar. Enjoy!

Lemony Carrot Cake with Cream Cheese Glaze

Ingredients

12 tbsp. margarine or butter, room temperature
3/4 cup packed light brown sugar
3 eggs
2 cups shredded carrots
1/3 cup raisins

1/3 cup coarsely chopped walnuts
Grated zest of 1 lemon
1 1/2 cups self-rising flour
1 tsp. baking powder
1/4 tsp. salt
Cream Cheese Glaze (recipe follows)

Method

Beat the margarine and brown sugar in large bowl until fluffy; beat in eggs one at a time, beating well after each addition. Mix in the carrots, raisins, walnuts, and lemon zest. Fold in a mixture of the flour, baking powder and salt. Pour the batter into a greased and floured 7-cup spring form pan; place on rack in slow cooker. Cover and cook on high until toothpick inserted in the center of cake comes out clean, about 31/2 hours. Cool pan on wire rack 10 minutes; remove side of pan and cool. Drizzle cake with Cream Cheese Glaze. Enjoy!

Cream Cheese Glaze

Makes about 3/4 cup

Ingredients

2 ounces reduced-fat cream cheese, room temperature
1 tbsp. margarine or butter, room temperature
1/2 tsp. vanilla
1 1/2 cups powdered sugar
Milk

Method

Beat the cream cheese, margarine, and vanilla in medium bowl until smooth; beat in powdered sugar and enough milk to make thick glaze consistency. Enjoy!

Pumpkin Ginger Cake Rounds with Warm Rum Sauce

Ingredients

1/2 cup canned pumpkin
½ cup packed light brown sugar
1/4 cup room temperature margarine or butter
¼ cup light molasses
1 egg
1 1/2 cups all-purpose flour

1/2 tsp. baking powder
½ tsp. baking soda
½ tsp. ground allspice
½ tsp. cloves
½ tsp. ginger
Warm Rum Sauce (recipe follows)

Method

Combine the pumpkin, brown sugar, margarine, molasses, and egg in large mixer bowl; beat at medium speed until well blended. Mix in combined flour, baking powder, baking soda, allspice, cloves, and ginger, blending at low speed until moistened. Pour batter into two greased and floured 16-ounce cans. Stand cans in slow cooker; cover and cook on high until wooden skewer inserted in the cakes comes out clean, for about 2 1/2 hours. Stand cans on wire rack to cool 10 minutes. Loosen sides of cakes by gently rolling cans on counter, or remove bottom ends of cans and push cakes through. Slice and serve with Warm Rum Sauce. Enjoy!

Warm Rum Sauce

Makes 1 1/2 cups

Ingredients

1/4 cup sugar
1 tbsp. cornstarch
11/4 cups 2% reduced-fat milk
2 tbsp. rum or 1/2 tsp. rum extract
2 tbsp. margarine or butter
1/2 tsp. vanilla
1/8 tsp. ground nutmeg

Method

Mix sugar and cornstarch in small saucepan; whisk in the milk and rum. Whisk over medium heat until the mixture boils and thickens, takes about 1 to 2 minutes. Remove from heat; stir in margarine, vanilla, and nutmeg. Serve warm.
Variation
Date and Nut Ginger Slices—Make the recipe as above, adding 1/4 cup each: chopped dates and walnuts; omit Warm Rum Sauce. Spread cake slices with softened cream cheese and apricot preserves. Enjoy!

Gingerbread Cake

Ingredients

1 1/2 cups self-rising flour
1/2 cup all-purpose flour
1 tsp. ground cinnamon
1/2 tsp. ground ginger
1/4 tsp. ground allspice
¼ tsp. salt
8 tbsp. margarine or butter, room temperature

2/3 cup light molasses
3/4 cup packed light brown sugar
1 egg, lightly beaten
1/2 cup 2% reduced-fat milk
1/2 tsp. baking soda
Cream Cheese Glaze (Recipe given earlier)

Method

Combine the flours, spices, and salt in large bowl. Combine the margarine, molasses, and brown sugar in 4-cup glass measure; microwave on high until margarine is melted, about 2 minutes, stirring to blend. Whisk margarine mixture into flour mixture, blending well; whisk in the egg. Whisk in combined milk and baking soda until blended. Pour batter into greased and floured 7-inch spring form pan; place on rack in slow cooker. Cover and cook on high until toothpick inserted in center of cake comes out clean, about 5 hours. Cool in pan on wire rack 10 minutes; remove side of pan and cool. Drizzle with cream cheese glaze. Enjoy!

Applesauce Cake with Buttery Glaze

Ingredients

1/2 cup margarine or butter, room temperature
3/4 cup packed light brown sugar
1 egg
3/4 cup applesauce
1 tsp. vanilla
1 cup all-purpose flour

1/2 cup whole-wheat flour
2 tsp. baking powder
1/2 tsp. salt
1/2tsp. ground cinnamon
1/4 tsp. each: baking soda, ground cloves
Buttery Glaze (recipe follows)

Method

Beat margarine and sugar in large bowl until blended; beat in the egg, apple-sauce, and vanilla. Mix in the remaining ingredients, except Buttery Glaze, stirring until well blended. Pour the batter into greased and floured 6-cup fluted cake pan; place pan on rack in 6-quart slow cooker. Cover and cook on high until toothpick inserted in center of cake comes out clean, 21/2 to 3 hours. Cool cake on wire rack 10 minutes; invert onto rack and cool. Enjoy!

Buttery Glaze

Makes about 1/3 cup

Ingredients

1 cup powdered sugar
1/2 tsp. butter extract
Milk

Method

Mix powdered sugar and butter extract with enough milk to make a glaze consistency. Enjoy!

Red Velvet Cake

Ingredients

3/4 cup sugar
3 tbsp. vegetable shortening
1 egg
1 tsp. vanilla

1 bottle (1 ounce) red food color
1/4 cup unsweetened cocoa
1 cup plus 2 tbsp. all-purpose flour
1 tsp. baking soda

1/2 tsp. salt
1/2 cup low-fat buttermilk

11/2 tsp. white distilled vinegar
Butter cream Frosting (recipe follows)

Method

Beat together the sugar and shortening until well blended in large bowl. Add egg and vanilla, blending well; beat in food color and cocoa until well blended. Mix in the mixture of flour, baking soda, and salt alternately with the mixture of buttermilk and vinegar, beginning and ending with dry ingredients. Pour the batter into greased and floured 1-quart soufflé dish; place on rack in 6-quart slow cooker. Cover and cook on high until toothpick inserted in center of cake comes out clean, 2 to 2 3/4 hours; remove to wire rack and cool for 10 minutes. Invert onto rack and cool; frost with Butter cream Frosting. Enjoy!

Butter cream Frosting

Ingredients

2 1/2 cups powdered sugar
1 tbsp. margarine or butter, room temperature
1/2 tsp. vanilla
1–2 tbsp. milk

Method

Mix powdered sugar, margarine, vanilla, and enough milk to make spreading consistency. Enjoy!

Chocolate Chip Peanut Butter Cake

Ingredients

1/3 cup room temperature margarine or butter
1/3 cup granulated
1/3 cup packed light brown sugar
2 eggs
1/2 cup chunky peanut butter

½ cup reduced-fat sour cream
1 2/3 cups self-rising flour
1/4 tsp. salt
1/2 cup semi-sweet chocolate morsels
Hot fudge or chocolate sauce (optional)

Method

Beat the margarine and sugars in bowl until fluffy; beat in eggs and keep blending well. Mix in the peanut butter and sour cream; mix in flour, salt, and chocolate morsels. Pour the batter into a greased and floured 6-cup fluted cake pan; place on rack in 6-quart slow cooker. Cover and cook on high until toothpick inserted in center of cake comes out clean, 2 to 2 1/2 hours. Cool cake on wire rack for 10 minutes; invert onto rack and cool. Serve with hot fudge sauce. Enjoy!

Conclusion

CHOOSE THE RIGHT VEGETABLES

To get ideal the nutrition from your slow-cooked meal, pick heat-friendly vegetables. These vegetables, like carrots, broccoli, tomatoes, kale and cabbage, discharge a high amount of healthy vitamins and antioxidants, when cooked as compared to their crude partners. Since moderate cooking warms and cooks vegetables at a low temperature, the procedure evacuates fewer vitamins from these heat-friendly vegetables than boiling or simmering. Vegetables like spinach and cucumber, on the other hand, don't cook as well in slow cookers and may get soft and less nutritious.

TRAP STEAM

The most ideal approach to ensure that no nutrients escape from your vegetables in the slow cooker is to trap the steam. When you put the water or stock into the cooker with your vegetables, twofold check to verify the cover fits the pot as hard as could reasonably be expected. Check to verify there are no splits or openings through which the steam may escape, and fight the temptation to remove the lid during the cooking process. As your vegetables cook, any spilled vitamins will be saved in the juices instead of vanishing.

EAT THE BROTH

Consume the broth along with your vegetables to ensure you're getting a supper that is as supplement rich as could reasonably be expected. When you remove your veggies from the slow cooker and strain out the water they were cooked in, you trick yourself and your family out of the profits of vitamins like vitamin C, which effectively drain into cooking water. If you need a slow-cooked meal abundant in veggies, take a try at making a soup or stew. Along with giving a simple to-set up one pot dinner, you will additionally ensure that your family receives the sum of the dietary profits vegetables give. You can additionally hold the vitamin-stuffed cooking water for utilization in a sauce or marinade, to go hand in hand with your supper, or as a soup base.

USE THE LOWEST SETTING

Cook your vegetables on your slow cooker's lowest setting to help keep vitamins, minerals and antioxidants locked inside. On most slow cooking devices, the lowest setting will cook your food at about 200 degrees Fahrenheit. Cooking a meal on the low setting takes a few hours longer, so you will need to plan ahead. Assemble the ingredients in your slow cooker in the morning, for instance, and come home from work hours later to a fully-cooked stew, soup or casserole.

Thank you again for purchasing this book!

Finally, if you enjoyed this book, please take the time to share your thoughts and post a review on Amazon. It'd be greatly appreciated!

Feel free to contact me at emma.katie@outlook.com

Check out more books by Emma Katie at:

www.amazon.com/author/emmakatie